"I HATE TO WRITE!"

"I HATE TO WRITE!"

**Tips for Helping Students
With Autism Spectrum and Related Disorders
Increase Achievement,
Meet Academic Standards, and
Become Happy, Successful Writers**

**Cheryl Boucher, MSEd, OTR,
and
Kathy Oehler, MS, CCC-SLP**

APC
PUBLISHING

P.O. Box 23173
Shawnee Mission, Kansas 66283-0173
www.aapcpublishing.net

©2013 AAPC Publishing
P.O. Box 23173
Shawnee Mission, Kansas 66283-0173
www.aapcpublishing.net

Publisher's Cataloging-in-Publication

Boucher, Cheryl.

"I hate to write!" : tips for helping students with autism spectrum and related disorders increase achievement, meet academic standards, and become happy, successful writers / Cheryl Boucher, and Kathy Oehler. – Shawnee Mission, Kan. : AAPC Publishing, c2013.

p. ; cm.

ISBN: 978-1-937473-11-2
LCCN: 2012953243
Includes bibliographical references.
Summary: Writing strategies developed specifically to address the issues faced by individuals with autism spectrum and related disorders.–Publisher.

1. Autistic children–Education–Study and teaching. 2. Children with autism spectrum disorders–Education–Study and teaching. 3. English language–Composition and exercises–Study and teaching. 4. English language–Rhetoric–Study and teaching. 5. Literacy–Study and teaching. 6. Teachers of children with disabilities–Handbooks, manuals, etc. I. Oehler, Kathy. II. Title.

LC4717.85 .B68 2013
371.94–dc23   1301

Cover art: ©iStockphoto

This book is designed in Frutiger.

Printed in the United States of America.

Dedication

This book is dedicated to Cheryl's nephew Casey Davis.
Casey is an amazing 14-year-old boy
with wonderful strengths.
Casey has taught his family far more than
any book or class could provide.

Table of Contents

Introduction

Most students on the autism spectrum hate to write. Even a simple writing assignment can trigger a major meltdown. Why does this happen? Why is the writing process so difficult for individuals on the autism spectrum? What can a parent or teacher do to help?

This book, written primarily for teachers and others who work with students with autism spectrum disorders (ASD), attempts to answer these questions. *"I HATE TO WRITE!"* examines the process of writing through the eyes of a person on the autism spectrum. Written by a speech-language pathologist and an occupational therapist with over 30 years of experience working with students with ASD, the book addresses the tremendous impact writing challenges can have on student behavior as well as on students' ability to achieve academic standards. With reference to current research on brain functioning, the authors explain why the process of writing is often so difficult for individuals with ASD. The authors also examine various writing tasks that are required in the school setting in order for students to achieve the National Common Core State Standards. Finally, the authors provide a wealth of simple strategies that can be implemented by teachers and others to help students meet these needs and become happy, successful writers.

Why Is Writing Such a Big Deal?

- *Writing demands can have a major impact on student behavior.* When asked to write, students with ASD often express extreme frustration because it's hard for them to put their ideas on paper. As part of school behavior support teams, the authors are often called in to help analyze and address severe behavior problems of students with ASD.   A major component of behavior intervention is the functional behavior analysis, which involves looking at, among other things, the antecedents (triggers) of behaviors.

  In the authors' experience, the most frequent trigger of behavior outbursts in the schools is a "request to do work." What does a "request to do work" usually mean? Write something! Even simple writing tasks require skills in areas that are often very difficult for individuals with ASD: language, organization, sensory regulation, and motor control. When students are asked to write, challenges in these areas often lead to refusal, negative behavior, or even meltdowns. *"I HATE TO WRITE!"* helps teachers recognize these behavior triggers and implement simple strategies to reduce behavior meltdowns when students are asked to write.

- *Writing demands can have a huge impact on a student's ability to meet academic standards.* After the middle of second grade, written output is the way schools most frequently measure academic proficiency. Until the middle of second grade, students often have the option of verbally telling the teacher what they know. But after that, academic achievement and proficiency is usually measured through tests or written assignments. Even when these are done electronically using a keyboard, the language, organization, sensory, and motor requirements of writing are still required.

The authors have sat in many conferences, including high school case conferences, where someone at the table says about a student, *"He has good intelligence and wonderful ideas, but I'm afraid he's not going to graduate because he never does his work. He didn't do his English book report, his history research paper, or his science lab report, and on his tests, he only writes the bare minimum."* What is the common denominator in each of these tasks? Writing!

Why Is the Writing Process so Difficult for Students With ASD?

The human brain is a very complicated mechanism. Each area of the brain has a primary function as well as many subsidiary duties. The key to making this brain machine work efficiently is the "wiring" – the neural connections that allow the various parts of the brain to communicate with each other.

Until recently, medical science believed that ASD affected only those areas of the brain that controlled social interactions, communication, and problem solving. However, with the advent of brain imaging, new information has emerged. For example, recent brain research has shown that there are significant differences in how the brains of individuals with ASD function. The most important difference appears to be in the way the various areas of the brain communicate with each other. In an autistic brain, messages don't get sent from one section of the brain to another with the same frequency and efficiency as they do in a neurotypical brain. The "parts" often work well, but they don't "talk" with each other!

This poor communication between key areas of the brain has a dramatic impact on the ability to write as the writing process requires a very high level of coordination between the various parts of the brain. In order to write, a person must activate the areas of the brain that govern motor control, language skills, sensory feedback, problem solving, imitation skills, memory, organization, and proprioception. But the real key to success is the ability of each area of the brain to let the other areas know what it is doing. For this to happen, thousands of neural signals must be sent back and forth throughout the brain.

The brain of a person with ASD appears to send far fewer of these coordinating neural messages. The result may be compared to a group of people crowded into a room, all working intently on the same project but never letting anyone know what they are doing. This would be inefficient and very frustrating, much like the writing process for a person with ASD.

The implications of current brain research are extremely important to educators who are teaching writing skills. Because the areas of their brains do not communicate efficiently with each other, most students with ASD have great difficulty coordinating all the skills needed for writing. The common response is *"I HATE TO WRITE!"*

But there are ways that a teacher can help. By providing simple supports to address the unique motor, sensory, language, and organizational challenges faced by individuals with ASD, a teacher can truly help a student with ASD become a successful, even happy, writer. And that is where this book comes in.

Teaching Strategies for Writing – Language, Organization, Sensory, Motor

As mentioned earlier, the process of writing involves language, organization, motor skills, and sensory processing. These four areas are problematic for many students with ASD, so it is essential to consider how they may be impacting a student's aversion to the writing process. However, no two students are alike, whether they have ASD or not. Therefore, the wise teacher will consider each of the potential problem areas and adapt the strategies to the particular needs of a given student.

In the past few years, much has been written about evidence-based practices (EBP) for autism, research-based interventions that can be used to promote specific outcomes for children with ASD. In 2009, the National Professional Development Center on Autism Spectrum Disorders released a list of 24 EBPs for children and youth with ASD. Many of the strategies included in *I Hate to Write!* reflect components of these practices. Wherever possible, the authors have referenced the correlation between writing strategy and evidence-based practice. A detailed description of the 24 evidence-based practices, as determined by the National Professional Development Center on Autism Spectrum Disorders, is available at: http://autismpdc.fpg.unc.edu/content/briefs. A second body of work regarding established treatments for individuals with ASD is available through the National Autism Center, National Standards Project 2009 (NAC 2009). This report may be accessed at http://www.nationalautismcenter.org/pdf/NAC%20Standards%20Report.pdf.

This manual provides practical strategies to support struggling writers. It is not intended to be an all-inclusive instructional textbook of sensory, language, fine-motor, and organizational strategies. Nevertheless, more detailed information about sensory processing is included in Appendix I. Please also consult your school speech-language pathologist or occupational therapist for additional strategies tailored specifically to your student.

How Can "I HATE TO WRITE!" Help?

"I HATE TO WRITE!" is written in user-friendly, "take it and use it" language. Each topic follows the following format:

 • **Teacher Concern:** Comments teachers often make regarding their students' writing difficulties

 • **Why:** A brief description of why students with ASD may display such difficulties and the impact it may have on student achievement, *including the research backing up the proposed strategies*

 • **Teaching Strategies:** Specific ideas for teachers to implement to help students meet the National Common Core Academic Standards (http://www.corestandards.org/)

 • **"Take It and Use It":** Printable pages of activities for teachers to use immediately

"I HATE TO WRITE!" is targeted toward teachers of students in grades K through 12. The strategies and "Take It and Use It" activities work for both beginning and intermediate writers. All strategies are designed to increase awareness of the unique challenges that a request to write places on individuals with ASD. The ultimate goal of this book is to help increase student achievement.

Gender Language

Throughout this book, the authors refer to the student with writing challenges as "he." This is not intended to indicate that boys corner the market on writing difficulties. However, it has been the experience of the authors that a disproportionate number of teacher cries for help are in reference to male students with ASD. Research suggests some possible reasons for this (see the research survey in Appendix A).

"Take It and Use It" Worksheets

The following series of worksheets and templates are designed to help students with ASD become happy, successful writers. In choosing topics, the authors have tried to address the most common writing requirements faced by students and teachers. Some worksheets are designed for elementary-age students, while others are more appropriate for older students.

Some of the "Take It and Use It" worksheets are designed for the teacher/parent to use as they support students during writing activities. Many of the worksheets include Teacher Instructions as well as Student Instructions. These instructions are intended to serve as suggestions for ways in which the worksheet can be used. These instructions can be deleted or revised, according to the need of the student. All of the worksheets may be downloaded by going to www.aapcpublishing.net/9078.

While the "Take It and Use It" worksheets are linked with specific tasks in this book, many of the strategies work for a variety of writing challenges. It is our hope that teachers will adapt and tweak the activities to make them appropriate for the individual student. Finally, the chart on pages 8-9 cross-references all strategies presented in this book for ease in planning.

> Throughout, general supports and strategies are marked with an asterisk (*) to indicate that a more detailed description is found in the Glossary in Appendix B.

National Common Core State Standards

Writing is now a high-stakes skill. On June 2, 2010, the National Governors Association and State Education Chiefs launched the National Common Core State Standards. The mission was to provide a consistent, clear understanding of what students attending schools in the United States are expected to learn. At the time of this writing, 46 states have accepted these Common Core Standards for use at the state level. Students are expected to show proficiency in each of the Common Core State Standards in order to graduate from high school. Many of the standards include a writing component. If a student cannot or won't write, therefore, that student will have difficulty achieving the Common Core Standards.

Throughout "I HATE TO WRITE!" the authors have linked writing challenges and strategies to the related Common Core State Standard. Students with ASD will have a much greater chance of achieving the standards when teachers implement the strategies suggested here. For further information on the Common Core State Standards, go to http://www.corestandards.org/.

Technology Tools for Writing

Throughout this manual the authors refer to the use of assistive technology (AT). IDEA, the Individuals with Disabilities Education Act (http://idea.ed.gov), defines assistive technology as "any item, piece of equipment, or product system … that is used to increase, maintain or improve functional capabilities of individuals with disabilities."

Assistive technology* supports for writing can be as simple as a pencil grip or as high tech as a word prediction* software program to support language and spelling. The right AT supports can make a world of difference for a student who struggles with the writing process. AT programs can provide visual cues to support students with language processing difficulties. AT programs can provide a wide variety of supports for students who struggle with organization. AT programs can support students with motor concerns by reducing the need for fine-motor control. And AT can help address sensory needs by, for example, reducing the number of keystrokes required to generate text (2000-2005 Assistive Technology Training Online Project).

We distinguish between two major categories of AT, low tech and high tech. Low-tech items may include something as simple as a pencil grip or a visual timer* to keep a student on track. High tech may include a tape recorder or a writing software program with computer access.

Strategies to Reverse the Common Student Complaint, "I HATE TO WRITE!"

At-a-Glance Cross-Referencing

"Take It and Use It" Worksheets

"Take It and Use It"	Strategies May Also Be Used With ...
Getting Started: #1: Writing Warm-Ups #2: Big-Muscle Warm-Ups	All topics
Knowing What to Write: #3: Picture Prompts/Make It Concrete! #4: Visual Timeline	Knowing What to Write, Getting "Stuck" When Writing, Getting Frustrated When Writing, Organizing a Paragraph, Writing the Bare Minimum, Thinking in Pictures
Choosing a Topic to Write About: #5: Building a Topic Library #6: Favorite Topic Writing Grid	Getting Started, Getting "Stuck" When Writing, Refusing to Write, Writing the Bare Minimum
Getting "Stuck" When Writing: #7: Story Frame #8: Pictures With Numbers	Getting Started, Choosing a Topic to Write About, Refusing to Write, Writing Paragraphs That Flow, Writing the Bare Minimum, Writing With Description, Thinking in Pictures, Writing a Book Report
Getting Frustrated When Writing: #9: Writing Warm-Ups – Sensory	All topics
Refusing to Write: #10: Brain Gym®	All topics
Writing It Down: #11: Spacer #12: Writing Warm-Ups – Big Muscle	Writing Legibly
Writing Legibly: #13: Desk Reminder – Writing Rules #14: Hand Exercises – Ready to Write! #15: Laser Power Letters	All topics
Understanding or Hearing Directions: #16: First/Then Visual Support #17: My Jobs	All topics
Misunderstanding Directions: #18: What We Say ...What They Hear	All topics
Spelling Words: #19: American Sign Language Alphabet	All topics
Organizing Words Into Sentences: #20: Out-of-Order Sentences	Getting Started, Getting Frustrated When Writing, Refusing to Write

"Take It and Use It"	Strategies May Also Be Used With ...
Writing Complete Sentences: #21: Say It, Glue It, Write It #22: Who, What, Where	Getting Started, Getting "Stuck" When Writing, Writing the Bare Minimum, Thinking in Pictures, Writing With Description
Organizing a Paragraph: #23: Keyword Story Web #24: Film Strip Paragraph	Getting Frustrated When Writing, Refusing to Write, Getting "Stuck" When Writing, Refusing to Write
Writing Paragraphs That Flow: #25: Write Your Keywords #26: Build a Burger Paragraph	Getting Frustrated When Writing, Refusing to Write, Getting "Stuck" When Writing, Organizing a Paragraph, Writing the Bare Minimum
Writing the Bare Minimum: #27: What Do I Do? #28: Address Sensory Needs = Write More!	All topics
Writing With Description: #29: Story Framework With Word Bank	Getting Frustrated When Writing, Refusing to Write, Getting "Stuck" When Writing, Organizing a Paragraph, Writing the Bare Minimum, Knowing What to Write
Writing and Editing: #30: Editing Checklist	All topics
Thinking in Pictures: #31: Storyline	Getting "Stuck" When Writing, Writing the Bare Minimum, Writing It Down, Getting Frustrated When Writing, Refusing to Write
Writing a Book Report: #32: Check for Understanding – Idioms #33: Book Report Template	All topics
Writing a Lab Report: #34: Lab Report/Scientific Method Template	Writing a Lab Report
Writing a Research Paper: #35: Research Paper Template: Elementary #36: Research Paper Template: Secondary	Writing a Research Paper
Writing a Letter: #37: Writing a Letter Template With Visual Choices	Writing a Letter

Getting Started

National Common Core State Standards for Writing:
Write routinely over extended time frames (time for research, reflection, and revision) and shorter time frames (a single sitting or a day or two) for a range of tasks, purposes, and audiences.

 Teacher Concern:
"When I give him a writing assignment, he just sits there. Even when it's an easy task, well within his ability, he seems to freeze."

Why:
A very-high functioning student with ASD recently told us, *"Even when I am highly motivated, and know what to do and how, I still don't do it. Instead, I sit and think about it or plan exactly what I am going to do in minute detail. I am stuck in inertia."*

Inertia is defined as *resistance or disinclination to motion, action, or change.* Scientifically, inertia appears to be a function of the neurological processes that control a person's ability to shift attention and plan voluntary motor movements. When a person has difficulty in these two areas, the result is often a tendency to stay still – to remain in a state of inertia (Donnelan, Hill, & Leary, 2010). Research on the brain functioning of individuals with ASD suggests that there is poor communication between the neurological areas that govern these skills (Herbert et al., 2004). In the case of writing, inertia describes the great difficulty many individuals have with beginning writing assignments.

Teaching Strategies:
Change the environment BEFORE the student begins writing. The EBP of antecedent-based intervention (ABI) indicates that this will increase on-task behavior (Luiselli, 2008).

Sensory:

Prior to starting the writing process:

- Ask the student to "quickly" deliver a message to a class at the end of the hall. Before he comes back to class, have him perform 30 wall push-ups.
- Ask the student to pass out papers or clean the dry-erase board.
- Reduce any auditory or visual distractions.
- Provide a visual check-off list for the student to follow.
- Allow the student to chew gum to help him regulate his sensory system.
- Allow the student to stand at his desk or kneel on his seat.
- Let the student listen to music with a quick beat as a way to break his tendency toward inertia.
- Allow the student to keep a water bottle at his desk.

Motor:

- In order to break the inertia for a younger student, provide hand-over-hand support* for the first written word of the assignment. With each letter of the word, keep your hand in place, but slowly fade the pressure of your hand on the student's hand. When you feel that the student has begun to write, slowly fade the presence of your hand. Often, this minimal physical prompt is enough to break the cycle of inertia and allow the student to proceed with the assignment on his own. Another suggestion involves applying light pressure, with the teacher's hand placed over the students helping hand. This is the hand that is holding the paper stationary. This may also help start the writing process. Once the student starts writing, remove your hand.
- In order to break the inertia for the older student, try having the student move from his regular desk and go to a writing table in the back of the room.
- Offer the student an opportunity to brainstorm out loud his ideas with the teacher or peer to get his thoughts rolling. Asking him to read a short essay may also assist his thoughts in moving in the right direction for his writing.

Organization:

- Use a graphic organizer* with pictures to break the inertia pattern. The brain has a terrific capacity to store pictures, particularly for those with ASD. (EBP – *Visual Support*)
- Chunk information.* The brain works best when we chunk information, which is what a graphic organizer provides. Sequence, brainstorm, and organize. The visual cues of a graphic organizer may greatly support the student's processing needs in moving to the next step in the writing process.

Technology:

- Many software programs offer graphic organizers.* Here is a sampling to check out: *Kidspiration* (www.kidspiration.com), *Inspiration* (www.inspiration.com), and *Draftbuilder* (www.donjohnston.com). Several other options are listed in Appendix H. (EBP – *Computer-Aided Instruction*)

    See also the following "Take It and Use It" worksheets: *#5 Building a Topic Library, #6 Favorite Topic Writing Grid, #7 Story Frame, #20 Out-of-Order Sentences, #21 Say It, Glue It, Write It, #22 Who, What Where.*

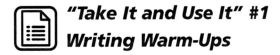

"Take It and Use It" #1
Writing Warm-Ups

Teacher Instruction: *Have the student keep this reminder in his writing folder. Ask him to do his four writing warm-ups before every writing assignment.*

Writing Warm-Ups – Ready to Work

Name: _____ **Date:** _____

Before I start my writing assignment, I will ...

	Push my hands together and release 10 times. Rub my hands on my legs 10 times.
	Open and close my fingers 10 times.
	Place my hands on the chair seat and then raise my bottom off of the seat 10 times.
	Breathe in slowly through my nose and then blow out through my lips. Repeat 5 times.

"Take It and Use It" #2
Big-Muscle Writing Warm-Ups

Teacher Instruction: *The following are big-muscle activities that may assist with motor control for writing and self-regulation to enhance attention and focus. Select activities from this list to provide your student with a 5- to 10-minute "job" before he has to start writing. For some students, the teacher or occupational therapist must determine which of these sensory jobs to implement, but for other students, the opportunity to self-select sensory strategies will increase compliance and owner-ship. Narrow them down to two or three choices that are reasonable for your school schedule and then allow him to pick. We suggest that the same job be used daily for a month. Then the following month, assist the student with choosing a new job.*

Assignment:

Name: _____ **Date:** _____

Before I start my writing assignment, I will _____
to help me wake up and improve my attention:

Choose One Warm-Up	WRITING WARM-UPS – Before I write, I will:
	Clean the dry-erase board or chalkboard
	Wipe tables in the cafeteria
	Collect/push the trash cans or recycling
	Return books to media center
	Run in gym or around track
	Fill crate with books to transfer back and forth to classrooms
	Assist gym teacher prep for classes
	Jump on a mini-trampoline
	Use hand weights/exercise in resource room or nurse's office
	Deliver a message to the office
	Complete 20 wall push-ups and 20 jumping jacks

Knowing What to Write

National Common Core State Standards for Writing:
Write narratives to develop real or imagined experiences or events using effective technique, descriptive details, and clear event sequences.

 Teacher Concern:
"He has good ideas, but when it's time to write, he can't think of anything to say."

Why:
Almost everybody who has an ASD, even those with very high abilities, has trouble understanding abstract concepts (Grandin, 1995). They have difficulty with instructions such as, "Take out your journal and write about anything you are interested in" or "Write about your favorite season." In order to understand what you want them to write about, students need instructions that are very concrete (Dodd, 2005).

There is a strong connection between our vestibular system and our language center (Ayres, 1979). The vestibular system controls our equilibrium, balance, both sides of our bodies working together, holding our head and neck up against gravity, and coordinating our eyes and hands working together. The vestibular system is activated with movement. So when we encourage movement, we may also be engaging the language center.

 Teaching Strategies:

Sensory:

- Allow the student a "pacing area." Identify an area of the room where the student can walk back and forth whenever he (or the teacher!) thinks he might need to move. Often this pacing action will have multiple benefits – it provides a movement break, it breaks the pattern of inertia, it activates the language centers of the brain, and it helps the student organize his thoughts.

- Provide time for a fast-paced walk in the hall or 2 minutes of jumping on a mini-trampoline before starting the writing process. This is a good way to alter the environment and increase attention and focus (Luiselli, 2008). (EBP – *Antecedent-Based Intervention*)

- For a quick fix, try a piece of sugarless gum. It works!

Language:

- Use pictures. Creative thought, as required in assignments involving imagination, prediction, and problem solving, can be very difficult for individuals with ASD, even those with high abilities. Photographs, line drawings, pictures from a textbook – all of these visual supports can help a student generate ideas for writing. (EBP – *Visual Supports*)

- Be specific. If you want the student to write about his favorite season, show him four seasonal pictures. Ask, "Which one is your favorite?" Have him write his answer on the paper. He now has a title. Ask him some concrete questions about what he likes to do in that season, how the air feels, what clothes he wears, etc. His answers to these concrete questions will become his list of ideas for writing. Allow the student to draw a picture of the beginning idea. This may support him visually while he expands on his descriptive writing.

- If the student is writing about a personal memory, ask him to close his eyes and "make a picture." Have him tell you what he "sees." What color, how big, etc. Expand by asking him more details.

- Show the student examples of what you are requesting. Whenever possible, relate the topic to an experience that is familiar to the student. You may need to help him recognize the link between his own experience and the assignment.

Motor: The student may have good ideas, but when he has to demonstrate other skills that are needed for "getting it on the paper," it may limit what and how much he shares. The language strategies provided may make the motor much more manageable. Also …

- Allow him to dictate his thoughts. This may give him the confidence to know he "can do it!" Then he can copy and add to the writing.

- Review the type of journal notebook the student is using. Would he do better if you provided a journal with fewer lines on the paper, larger lines, highlighted lines, or even graphing paper* for letter placement? Creating a personal spiral-bound journal* takes just a few minutes.

- Give the student closure on how many sentences he has to write. A task can become much more manageable when the student knows "how much."

Organization:

- Use key words. Ask the student to tell you about the topic. For each sentence that the student says, write down a keyword. This list of keywords becomes the outline for writing.

- Use a visual timeline. If the assignment involves writing about an event, draw a line at the top of the paper. Ask the student what happened first. Draw a simple line drawing (or write a keyword) at the left end of the timeline. Ask him what happened next. Write or draw another reminder slightly to the right. Continue adding items to the timeline until the student has enough items in the sequence for a story. Then number the pictures. Have the student write a sentence for each numbered picture.

Technology:

- Try using a computer/keyboard. As an added support, type three or four concrete sentence starters related to the topic on the student's screen. Besides reducing the need for paper-pencil output, this type of support gives the student two additional benefits: It helps address the challenge of knowing what to write, and it also helps the student "chunk"* his writing into a more organized format. Try taking turns typing. This can ease the student into the writing without stress. "I type a sentence, and then you type a sentence." (EBP – Computer-Aided Instruction)

See also the following "Take It and Use It" worksheets: #1 *Writing Warm-Ups, #2 Big-Muscle Warm-Ups, #8 Pictures With Numbers, #9 Writing Warm-Ups – Sensory, #12 Writing Warm-Ups – Big Muscle, #28 Address Sensory Needs = Write More!, #31 Storyline.*

"Take It and Use It" #3
Picture Prompts Make It Concrete!

Name: _____ Date: _____

Assignment: *Write a story about your favorite season.*

| SPRING | SUMMER | FALL | WINTER |

1. **My favorite season is:**_____ (Title)

2. **In _____ the air feels:** _____

3. **In _____ the weather is:**_____

4. **In _____ I wear:** _____

5. **In _____I like to:** _____

6. **That is fun because:** _____

7. **Another thing I do in the _____ is:** _____

8. **I really like the season of:**_____

On a different sheet of paper, write a story about your favorite season. Use the words above to help you. Make your story at least eight sentences long.

"Take It and Use It" #4
Visual Timeline

Teacher prompt: *"Tell me about our trip to the apple orchard. What did we do first?"* *For each experience the child relates, draw a simple picture on the timeline. After the child has related enough items for a sequential story, number the pictures. Then ask the child to write a paragraph, with one sentence for each numbered picture.*

Name: _____ **Date:** _____

Assignment: *Write a story about visiting the apple orchard. Write one sentence for each picture.*

| 1 | 2 | 3 | 4 | 5 | 6 | 7 | 8 |

MY TRIP TO THE APPLE ORCHARD

1. _____

    _____ .

2. _____

    _____ .

3. _____

    _____ .

4. _____

    _____ .

5. _____

    _____ .

6. _____

    _____ .

7. _____

    _____ .

8. _____

    _____ .

Choosing a Topic to Write About

National Common Core State Standards for Language:
Write informative/explanatory texts to examine and convey complex ideas and information clearly and accurately through the effective selection, organization, and analysis of content.

Teacher Concern:
"When it's writing time, he can't come up with a topic. He seems to get stuck on the same one or two ideas. If he can't write about those topics, he doesn't write at all."

Why:
Simon Baron-Cohen, professor of Developmental Psychopathology at the University of Cambridge and director of the Autism Research Centre (ARC) in Cambridge (Craig & Baron-Cohen, 1999), has written about the biology of imagination in the brain of a person with ASD. Baron-Cohen explains that imagination is very complex. The act of imagination involves making a visual image of something real, and then generating ideas of how that image could be changed into something new and different. This ability to generate novel ideas is very challenging for individuals with ASD (Williams & Minshew, 2010). Baron-Cohen's research indicates that biological differences in the brain are responsible for the difficulty that people with ASD have with generating imaginative ideas (Craig & Baron-Cohen).

When a student, particularly one with an ASD, has had hands-on experience (visual, auditory, tactile, olfactory, taste) that was meaningful to him, he becomes more engaged in the process (Wade, 2008). A writing prompt requesting students to write about a warm summer day may not be a good choice. Just because many of us enjoy all of the sensory experiences of a lovely summer day, that may not be the case for an individual with ASD (Brown & Dunn, 2010). A student with ASD may not have registered the sensory components, or he may be overly sensitive to the feel of a warm breeze or the brightness of the sunshine. However, the same student loved flying a paper airplane on a windy day – a hands-on experience. He was then able to write about how high and how far the airplane flew. When he has experienced the subject, the writing is more successful.

Individuals with ASD thrive on consistency, routine, and sameness (Fein, 2011). This innate desire for consistency is often reflected in a student's writing choices. Without encouragement and guidance from a teacher, the student will almost always revert to a familiar, comfortable topic.

Teaching Strategies:

Organization:

- Pick your battles. If your goal is for the student to actually write, allow him to write about his area of intense interest. You can broaden the options within the area of intense interest by helping him develop a list of various aspects of this favorite topic. Each writing session can then focus on that particular aspect. Remember, he can progress with learning the various writing standards through his high-interest areas. He may give you five paragraphs on a preferred topic instead of only five sentences on a topic that he has little to no interest in. Or if he has not experienced the topic and, therefore, lacks a visualization of the topic, he will likely write less. As his writing skills progress, branching out into more diverse topics will be more successful. (EBP – *Antecedent-Based Intervention*)

  If your goal is to broaden his range of writing, do some preparation work with the student. Spend an entire writing session developing a list of topics for future writing sessions. Use books or pictures to help the student visualize the possibilities. Keep the list of topics in his writing book. When it is time to write, he must choose from the list that has been prepared. This will allow future writing sessions to focus on the actual writing task, without wasting time trying to decide what to write about.

Language:

- Let a picture help generate the topic. Give the student three pictures of different types of activities. Ask which picture he wants to write about. After he has chosen, remove the other pictures. Have him write about what he sees in the picture. While imaginative thought might not be a particular strength, the student may amaze you with his attention to detail. (EBP – *Visual Supports*)

Sensory:

- Prior to writing, give the student a big-muscle job (heavy work*) to help him regulate his system so he can focus on writing. (EBP – *Antecedent-Based Intervention*)
- Tie some stretchy exercise band or tubing* to two of the desk legs. This simple strategy offers a great sensory regulator as the student feels the bounce and resistance of the stretchy band with his foot/leg. This allows him to get some lower leg movement without having to leave his desk.

Motor:

- Take turns writing sentences with the student. Let him dictate a sentence or two as you write, then pass the pencil or portable keyboard (see Appendix H) to him and have him write what you say. With some students, the repetitive phrases "My turn" and "Your turn" help them understand the reciprocal nature of the activity.

- Look at the way the student's body is positioned in his seat. Adjust, if necessary. Make sure the student is sitting squarely on the seat and that the seat is close enough to the desk to support a good writing posture. Check the height of the student's desk.* The student's legs must be able to fit under the desk, and the desk must be high enough to support the student's forearms as he sits. As a general rule, the desk should be two inches taller than a bent elbow that is flexed at 90 degrees.

- Check the desktop. Desks are frequently covered with "extras." Have him clear his desktop so that there is nothing on it except what he needs for the writing assignment.

- Remember that there is a strong chance that pencil-paper tasks are not the student's strength. Offer the use of a keyboard for the student who struggles with forming letters, a strained grasp, or poor quality of writing. See also Appendix D.

    See also the following "Take It and Use It" worksheets: #1 *Writing Warm-Ups*, #2 *Big-Muscle Warm-Ups*, #7 *Story Frame*, #10 *Brain Gym®*, #27 *What Do I Do?* #28 *Address Sensory Needs = Write More!*

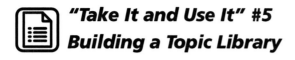

"Take It and Use It" #5
Building a Topic Library

Teacher Instructions: *Help the student develop a list of writing topics. Then help the student write a first sentence for each topic. Have the student keep this list in his writing folder. Future writing topics can be chosen from this list.*

Name: _____ **Date:** _____

Assignment: *Think of five topics you could write about. Write these topics on your paper. Then write one sentence about each of your topics. Keep this paper in your writing folder.*

I WILL WRITE ABOUT ...

TOPIC	FIRST SENTENCE

"Take It and Use It" #6
Favorite Topic Writing Grid (Example)

Teacher Instructions: *Use the student's area of intense interest as a source of writing topics. Help the student complete the grid, using various aspects of the interest as future writing topics. Help the student write a topic sentence for each idea. Have the student keep the grid in his writing folder where he can use it to choose new topics.*

Example:

I AM VERY INTERESTED IN *COMPUTERS*

I will write about:	First sentence:
My favorite computer game	My favorite computer game is *Sonic the Hedgehog*.
Our computer lab	There are 24 computers in our school computer lab.
The parts of a computer	A computer has many parts.
Our classroom computer rules	We have rules for using the computer in my classroom.

**"Take It and Use It" #6**
Favorite Topic Writing Grid

Name: _____ **Date:** _____

Assignment: *Choose a topic that is interesting to you. Choose five things about that topic that you could write about. Write one sentence for each of the five things.*

I AM VERY INTERESTED IN _____

I will write about:	First sentence:

Getting "Stuck" When Writing

National Common Core State Standards for Writing:
Write routinely over extended time frames (time for research, reflection, and revision) and shorter time frames (a single sitting or a day or two) for a range of tasks, purposes, and audiences.

 Teacher Concern:
"He gets 'stuck' when he is writing. He starts the assignment, but then gets stuck on one idea and can't seem to make himself move on."

 Why:
Several factors may be at work here.

- *Language processing*: Many students with ASD have slow processing skills, even if they have average and above intelligence. They "think in pictures" and then must translate those pictures into words that they can write down for the assignment. If they lose the "picture," they are stuck (Grandin, 2011).

- *Concrete thinking*: Most individuals with ASD are very concrete in their thinking. Imagination and creative thought are areas of weakness. This difficulty makes it hard to come up with new ideas (Amaral, Dawson, & Geschwind, 2011).

- *Perseverative thought*: Perseveration, or the tendency to repeat an idea or action over and over, is a common trait of ASD (Aman, Arnold, & Armstrong, 1999). In the writing process, this tendency makes it a challenge to transition from one idea or sentence to the next.

- *Perfectionism*: Students with ASD are often perfectionists (Ory, 2001). They may spend lots of time erasing or correcting work that isn't perfect to their way of thinking. They often become anxious or angry if their work doesn't look right to them. No amount of teacher assurance will eliminate this desire for precision.

Teaching Strategies:

Language:

- Provide the student with a list of starter sentences, adjectives, or transition phrases that he can plug into his writing. He can use material from this list when he gets stuck.
- Allow the student to keep a picture of his topic on his desk. With the teacher's help, he can write numbers on the picture, illustrating various ideas he could write about. If he gets stuck, he can use the numbered pictures as visual cues for writing. (EBP – *Visual Supports*)

Organization:

- Provide a story frame* in which you write sentence starters, transition words, adjectives, etc., at various places on the student's paper. These visual cues will help the student organize his thoughts as he writes.
- To address compulsive erasing, take away the student's eraser. Tell him he can circle any mistakes that he sees and then continue with the assignment. By providing a different way for the student to acknowledge his "imperfections," you may be able to break the erasing habit and help him keep working.

Sensory:

- Break the cycle of perseverating by directing the student to perform a quick functional task, such as ...
  - Wiping off the board
  - Taking a message to the office (EBP – *Antecedent-Based Intervention*)
  - Moving books to the back of the room
  - Standing and stretching up to the ceiling/down to the floor 10 times
  - Allowing the student the opportunity to squeeze a fidget* ball often provides enough sensory support to help break the cycle of perseveration

---

Motor/Technology:

- If a student has slow or illegible handwriting, it may be because he has visual motor challenges. When a student's visual motor skills are challenged, it is wise to reduce the paper-pencil requirement and allow him to write using a portable word processor, computer/keyboard, or tablet. Some students may be more successful with the large screen of a PC or laptop, while other students may benefit from fewer stimuli and the convenience of a portable word processor. Besides reducing the need to scribe perfect letters, the "delete" and "backspace" functions of a portable word processor eliminate the tendency toward compulsive erasing. Portable word processors have fewer bells and whistles than laptop computers. The simplicity and portability of this technology make it a good choice for many students with ASD. There are several types of portable keyboards on the market. See Appendix H for options. (EBP – *Computer-Aided Instruction*)

  See also the following "Take It and Use It" worksheets: *#1 Writing Warm-Ups, #2 Big-Muscle Warm-Ups, #10 Brain Gym®, #25 Write Your Keywords, #26 Build a Burger Paragraph, #27 What Do I Do?, #28 Address Sensory Needs = Write More!, #32 Check for Understanding – Idioms.*

"Take It and Use It" #7
Story Frame

Name: _____ **Date:** _____

Assignment: *Write about the story we just read.*

STORY FRAME

In this story, the problem began when _____

_____ .

After that, _____

_____ .

Next, _____

_____ .

Then, _____

_____ .

The problem is finally solved when _____

_____ .

The story ends _____

_____ .

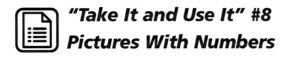 **"Take It and Use It" #8**
Pictures With Numbers

Name: _____ **Date:** _____

Assignment: *Write a story. Use the numbers on the picture to help you think of ideas.*

Getting Frustrated When Writing

National Common Core State Standards for Writing:
Write routinely over extended time frames (time for research, reflection, and revision) and shorter time frames (a single sitting or a day or two) for a range of discipline-specific tasks, purposes, and audiences.

 Teacher Concern:
"He knows that we write in our journals each morning, but as soon as he sees his journal, he has a meltdown."

Why:
The writing process requires students with ASD to do all the things that are hardest for them – focus their attention, organize their thoughts, generate an idea, hold a pencil, listen to the noise the pencil makes on the paper, write neatly, etc., etc. To make things even more frustrating, most students with ASD have some degree of fine-motor/coordination difficulty. When all these hard jobs are required at the same time, students may go into sensory overload, and sensory overload often results in frustration, refusal, and meltdown (Ayres, 2000).

So, if you have a student who becomes easily frustrated when it is time to do a writing task, give careful thought to exactly what you are trying to teach in that lesson. Help the student accomplish that one skill and let the other requirements of writing wait for another lesson. Several examples are listed in the following.

 **Teaching Strategies:**

Sensory:

Prior to any stage of the writing process:

- Offer a movement break. The student who appears "tired, lazy, unmotivated" may need his nervous system fired up. Ask him to pass out the papers, wipe off the dry-erase board, or send him to deliver a quick message to another class.

- Schedule in a heavy-work activity.*

- Position the student in a quiet area with limited visual distractions.

- Allow the student to stand at his area or sit in a beanbag chair with a clipboard. Let him choose which position he thinks will help him. He may grow to be his own best advocate in knowing what he needs for sensory regulation.

- Allow the student to chew a piece of sugarless gum. We have been impressed with how well a little jaw "work" assists in regulating a student and assisting with focus on a task! (See Appendix J.)

- Consider a reinforcer to be paired with the writing to initially avoid a meltdown. (EBP – *Reinforcement*)

- Position near a positive, supportive peer buddy.* (EBP – *Peer-Mediated Instruction*)

Language:

If you are trying to teach …

- *Writing about personal experiences:* Ask parents to send in several pictures of the student engaged in an activity at home. Keep the pictures at school. When it is time to write, have the student select one of the pictures to write about. Tell the student exactly how much he has to write.

- *Writing complete sentences:* Show the student a picture. Ask him to tell you one sentence about the picture. Count his words, holding up your fingers as you count. Ask the student how many words were in his sentence. Tell him to write his *six-word* sentence in his journal, starting with a capital letter and ending with a period.

Organization:

If you are trying to teach …

- *Organizing sentences into a well-sequenced paragraph:* Let the student dictate his sentences to you. Quickly write each sentence on a strip of paper. The student then pastes the sentences in order into his journal.

Motor:

If you are trying to teach …

Spacing between words:

- Let the student dictate his journal entry to you. You write it. Using your written model, his job is to copy his sentence WITH SPACES (see Appendix F) in his journal.

- Try using graph paper* to provide a visual cue of one letter per square and two squares between words.

Writing legibly:

- Encourage hand warm-up exercises prior to writing. Examples might include pressing the hands together ten times; opening a closing fists/ stretching fingers 10 times; rubbing hands on thighs 10 times.

- Try offering the use of a pencil grip* if your student holds the pencil *with all his fingers* or with the pencil held in the web space between the index finger and thumb.

- For younger students, let the student dictate his journal entry to you. You "dot letter" every other word in his sentence. His job is to write one word, then trace your dot word, then write one word, then trace, etc. Or after the student has dictated to you, he may then copy from the dictated thoughts.

- Check the student's journal. Many journals are spiral-bound notebooks. These are frequently too small with too many lines for students with ASD. Depending on your student's needs, try typing and copying your own lined paper with more space between lines and fewer lines on a page or download and print free copies from http://www.do2learn.com. These papers can easily be stapled, tied, or otherwise bound together into a journal. Remember for the left-handed writer, spiral journals add an extra challenge since the spiral is on the left side of the paper. Individualize the journal by placing the binding pages on the right side of the paper. This can easily be done by stapling, tying, or using a manual binder on the right-hand side of the paper. (See Appendix C.)

If you are trying to develop love of writing …

- Allow the student to use a keyboard. Skip paper-pencil.

- Allow the student to write about his favorite preferred topic. (EBP – *Antecedent-Based Intervention*)

- Provide a sense of closure by telling the student exactly how many sentences he has to write and what he can do when he has finished writing (see "Take It and Use It" #27). Use a visual timer* and ask the student to work until the red is gone or the timer sound goes off. He can even help to set the time to have a feeling of control.

- Consider pairing the task with a First/Then* card. That is, FIRST he writes, THEN he is allowed a short break or a reinforcer. (EBP – *Reinforcement*)

- Provide frequent praise for each little positive attempt. (EBP – *Reinforcement*)

    Also see the following "Take It and Use It" worksheets: *#3 Picture Prompts – Make It Concrete!, #4 Visual Timeline, #13 Desk Reminder – Writing Rules, #16 First/Then Visual Support, #17 My Jobs, #25 Write Your Keywords, #26 Build a Burger Paragraph, #27 What Do I Do?*

"Take It and Use It" #9
Writing Warm-Ups – Sensory

Teacher Instruction: *For some students, the teacher/occupational therapist will need to determine which of these sensory strategies should be implemented, but for other students the opportunity to self-select sensory strategies will increase compliance and ownership.*

If you allow the student to self-select, do the following: At the beginning of the day, have the student select three or four of these writing warm-ups for use that day. Make sure all options that you offer are available (a quiet desk area, etc.). Ask him to do his writing warm-ups before every writing assignment.

Writing Warm-Ups – Sensory

Name: _____   Date: _____

Before I start my writing assignment, I will …

Activity	What It Looks Like	How to Do It
Jumping jacks		20 jumping jacks Jump out with arms and legs, making an X; jump in legs together and arms at your side.
Seat push-ups		10 seat push-ups Push down hard with hands on chair seat; raise bottom off of chair using upper-body strength.
Wall push-ups		20 wall push-ups Stand with your feet away from the wall. Now, put your hands on the wall. Push away as hard as you can, like you are doing a push-up.
Beanbag chair		Beanbag chair Push the beanbag chair into a corner. Squish your body deep into the chair while you do your writing.
Headphones/ earplugs		Headphones/earplugs Wear headphones or earplugs every time you write today.
Chewing gum		Chewing gum Chew gum while you write today.
Drinking water		Water bottle Keep a water bottle on your desk while you write. Take a drink before you start writing and another drink when you need to stop and think during writing.
Quiet "office" space		Private office area Do your writing in your "private office area" today.
Fidget object	Squeeze, feel, self-regulate	10 squeezes Before you write, squeeze your squeeze ball 10 times with each hand. Squeeze hard! When you are thinking about what to write next, squeeze again.

Refusing to Write

National Common Core State Standards Anchor Skills for Writing:
Write routinely over extended time frames (time for research, reflection, and revision) and shorter time frames (a single sitting or a day or two) for a range of tasks, purposes, and audiences.

 Teacher Concern:"*When it's time to write, he won't even try.*"

 Why:
Sometimes a student's refusal to write is due to his need for perfection: Many individuals with ASD have an almost compulsive need for precision and perfection (De Boer, 2009). Because the act of writing involves so many skills that are difficult for persons on the autism spectrum (fine-motor control, ability to generate ideas, ability to organize and sequence, ability to filter out competing stimuli, etc.), the probability of perfection is slim. Some students with ASD repetitively erase their writing attempts in an effort to get them "perfect" until they rub holes in their papers. Such intense erasing is also a strong signal to the teacher that the student is moving to the refusal stage of writing. This is an appropriate time to consider other modalities for writing. In other words, move to the computer!

For other students with an ASD, a request to write may bring up unhappy memories of previous writing experiences involving physical and mental fatigue, frustration, being told to rewrite, receiving a poor grade, and more. This mindset of "writing = aversive situation" can cause refusal when it is time to pick up a pencil and write. To prevent this refusal from escalating into a problem behavior, the adult needs to implement some strategies to set the student up for success (Luiselli, 2008). Research has shown that problem behaviors can be prevented when aversive events are minimized (Horner, Carr, Strain, Todd, & Reed, 2002). Simple interventions like changing the writing environment or having the student do a brief exercise after every two sentences can make a huge difference in a student's willingness to write.

Finally, because writing presents so many challenges to students with ASD, every writing task seems endless and overwhelming. Students show more willingness to write when they can see EXACTLY how much they have to do (Hume & Odom, 2007).

Teaching Strategies:

Sensory:

- Set the student up for success. Provide a jump-start to get him engaged and to decrease anxiety. Ask him to perform some big-muscle movements. Twenty quick jumping jacks may do the trick.

  For older students, set up a daily job that can be performed before writing block, such as delivering a crate of books to the library.

- Give the student a choice of where to write: corner office, at an end computer with fewer stimuli, or even in the hall right outside the classroom. (EBP – *Antecedent-Based Intervention*)

- Have a water bottle handy. It can be a great brain energizer and self-regulating tool.

- Let the student write with a fine-tip marker or a gel pen. It makes less noise on paper than a pencil. Also, since the writing can't be erased, it reduces the cycle of compulsive erasing.

- Consider using a special visual timer* or simply a kitchen timer. For the student who doesn't want to write at all, visual closure can be helpful. The student helps set the timer for 15 minutes or a length of time that is reasonable for the student's needs and strengths.

- Try using a First/Then Card,* showing the child visually that first he writes and then he gets to have a break. Remember a reinforcer (What is he motivated to work on earning?) (EBP – *Reinforcement*)

Motor:

- Offer several writing tool options – a gel pen, scented pencil,* or a cushy pencil grip.*

- Show the student EXACTLY how much he has to write. If you want him to write four sentences, give him a paper with numbers 1-4 spaced evenly down the left side of the paper. This simple, concrete strategy helps give the student a sense of closure by showing him EXACTLY how much he needs to write.

- For the student who has difficulty with size and placement of letters, draw long boxes on each row next to the number and tell the student to write his words in the boxes. The student then visually knows where to print. See also Appendices D and F.

- For the student who writes too large or too small, define his visual writing area by using a yellow highlighter. The student writes over the yellow areas. See also Appendix D.

- If printing is a challenge, allow the student to use a keyboard for written assignments. A small portable keyboard (see Appendix H) is an inexpensive alternative. It weighs about two pounds and can be kept at the student's desk or carried in a backpack. The student will be able to experience the success of writing his thoughts without the frustration of imperfect letter formation. A portable word processor also provides a quick backspace button for easy erasing. Besides, it allows the student to clearly see the words he has created.

- **CELEBRATE** each little step towards success!!! (EBP – *Reinforcement*)

Language:

- Use a text-to-speech software program* (e.g., *Write: Outloud;* www.donjohnston.com). This type of software is widely available and relatively inexpensive. The student types a sentence, and the computer reads the sentence aloud. The program can be programmed to read each word, each sentence, or each paragraph, depending on the needs of the student. Besides allowing the student to hear whether or not his writing makes sense, the immediate feedback of hearing his words read aloud often provides enough motivation to keep the student writing. See also Appendix H. (EBP – *Computer-Aided Instruction*)

- Allow the student to choose one of his favorite topics. Remember we are trying to develop a love for writing.

- Give the student a picture to write about. Tell the student exactly how many sentences he has to write. These concrete cues will reduce the tendency toward writing refusal.

Organization:

- Use one of the computer-based graphic organizers* to help the student record his ideas. Graphic organizers can help a student organize a simple sentence or an entire term paper. (Most computer-based programs have text-to-speech capability, so the student can hear his ideas as soon as he types them. See Appendix H.)

- Allow the student to first brainstorm words and phrases that can be typed. He now has his "memory" of all his thoughts on the topic. Depending on skill level, either have him type as he brainstorms or have an adult assists with the typing. Either way, his ideas are on the computer screen to make the writing manageable.

- Consider using a software program for graphic organizing.* A particular favorite is SOLO with *Draft:Builder* (www.donjohnston.com) for brainstorming. The four programs in SOLO allow the writer to click and connect to each program. After the student brainstorms in *Draft:Builder,* he can click on a button, and the brainstorming is sent to *Write: OutLoud* (www.donjohnston.com). On the left side of the page will appear his brainstorming notes, and the rest of the page is ready with a talking word processor to complete the job. See also Appendix H. (EBP – *Computer-Aided Instruction*)

- Other graphic organizer* programs such as *Kidspiration* (www.kidspiration.com) for elementary students and *Inspiration* (www.inspiration.com) for older students provide the visual organization that many students need to have a positive feeling that "I can do it!"

  See also the following "Take It and Use It" worksheets: *#1 Writing Warm-Ups, #2 Big-Muscle Warm-Ups, #5 Building a Topic Library, #6 Favorite Topic Writing Grid, #8 Pictures With Numbers, #23 Keyword Story Web, #24 Film Strip Paragraph, #25 Write Your Keywords, #26 Build a Burger Paragraph, #27 What Do I Do?*

"Take It and Use It" #10
Brain Gym®

Teacher Instructions: *Have the entire class participate in Brain Gym® exercises before writing.*

The following exercises are reprinted with permission from 2010 Brain Gym® Teacher's Edition (Dennison, Paul E., & Gail E. Dennison. Brain Gym® Teacher's Edition. Edu-Kinesthetics, Inc., 2010).

Brain Gym® is a registered trademark of Brain Gym® International/Educational Kinesiology Foundation.

Brain Buttons Academic skills this activity may enhance: • Ease of eye movement when crossing the visual midline when reading • Crossing the midline for body coordination • Directionality for keeping one's place while reading, correct ordering of letters and numbers, and left to right scanning for improved consonant blending • Digital and hand-eye coordination for handwriting or computer work Behavioral/Postural Correlates • Left-right balance (hips level, head upright and centered • An enhanced energy level • Improved eye teaming skills (may alleviate visual stress, squinting or staring) • Greater relaxation of neck and shoulder muscles	To stimulate the brain buttons, make a U shape with one hand and place your thumb and index finger in the soft depressions just below your collarbones and to each side of your sternum, placing your other hand over your navel. Rub the brain buttons for 20-30 seconds (or until any tenderness is released), with your lower hand still, as you move your eyes slowly to the left and right along a horizontal line. Then switch hands and repeat the activity.
The Cross Crawl Academic skills this activity may enhance: • Spelling and writing • Listening • Reading and comprehension Behavioral/Postural Correlates • Improved left-right coordination • Ease of movement through counterbalancing of the limbs • Enhanced breathing and stamina • Improved listening and attention	Stand comfortably and reach across the midline of your body as you alternately move one arm and its opposite leg, then the other arm and leg, rhythmically touching each hand or elbow to the opposite knee.

The following exercises are reprinted with permission from 2010 Brain Gym® Teacher's Edition (Dennison, Paul E., & Gail E. Dennison. Brain Gym® Teacher's Edition. Edu-Kinesthetics, Inc., 2010).

Brain Gym® is a registered trademark of Brain Gym® International/Educational Kinesiology Foundation.

Hook-Ups: Academic skills this activity may enhance: • Clear listening and speaking • Test taking and similar challenges • Work at the keyboard Behavioral/Postural Correlates • Improved self-control and sense of boundaries • Enhanced balance and coordination • Increased comfort in the environment (less hypersensitivity) • Deeper respiration and improved circulation	**Part One:** Cross your ankles. Next extend your arms in front of you and cross one wrist over the other; then interlace your fingers and draw your clasped hands up toward your chest. Hold like this for a minute or more, breathing slowly, with your eyes open or closed. As you inhale, touch the tip of your tongue to the roof of your mouth at the hard palate (just behind the teeth), and relax your tongue on exhalation. **Part Two:** When ready, uncross you arms and legs and put your fingertips together in front of your chest, continuing to breathe deeply for another minute and hold the top of your tongue on the roof of your mouth when you inhale.
Arm Activation: Academic skills this activity may enhance: • Penmanship and cursive writing • Spelling • Creative writing Behavioral/Postural Correlates • A longer attention span for written work • Improved focus and concentration without overfocus • Improved postural alignment • An enhanced ability to express ideas • Improved hand-eye coordination and the facile manipulation of tools or musical instruments • Increased energy in the hands and fingers (relaxes writer's cramp) • Relaxed movement of the diaphragm and increased respiration	Sit or stand with your feet parallel and shoulder-width apart. Raise one arm above your head, using the opposite hand to hold it next to your ear. Exhale gently through pursed lips, while activating your muscles isometrically by pushing your raised arm against the other hand. Do this three times, exhaling each time to a count of eight. This activation is done in four directions: toward the head, forward, backward, and away from the head. Then repeat the process on the other side.

Writing It Down

National Common Core State Standards for Writing:
Write informative/explanatory texts to examine a topic and convey ideas and information clearly.

 Teacher Concern:
"He can verbalize his answers and thoughts, but he cannot get them written on to the paper."

Why:
Due to the multiple subskills – language, organization, sensory regulation, and motor control – required for successful writing, many factors may be involved in a student's difficulty getting ideas down on paper, including the following.

- Some students with ASD are very sensitive to sound or visual stimuli (Gray, 2008). For example, the sound of a pencil marking on paper may seem extremely loud and irritating to them. This may cause the student to avoid all tasks that involve writing with a pencil.

- Many students with ASD have challenges with fine-motor skills (Hamilton, n.d.). Holding, positioning, and grasping a pencil may be physically uncomfortable. This may cause the student to avoid tasks that involve holding a writing tool.

- Many students with ASD have difficulty with sequencing and organization (Gray, 2008). This difficulty is magnified during writing tasks, which require the student to block out sensory stimuli, position a pencil, organize thoughts, hold on to a working memory, and sequence letters on the page – all at the same time.

- Many students with ASD have trouble with phonemic awareness (Mirenda, 2003); that is, the ability to understand the relationship between sounds, letters, and symbols.

 **Teaching Strategies:**

> ### Sensory:
>
> If you suspect that a student might have difficulty filtering out sensory stimuli (visual, auditory, tactile, olfactory, or proprioceptive):
>
> - Provide a heavy work* movement break prior to seat work. (Carry a stack of books to the library. Clean the chalkboard. Do wall push-ups. Try jumping jacks.) This will help the student regulate his sensory system.
> - Provide a quiet "office" space where auditory and visual stimuli are reduced. View the area from the student's perspective. What visual distractions are in his view, do other students pass by the area? Are there chatty peers who are not following the quiet rule? Careful development of a functional behavior analysis will help identify underlying triggers for work refusal and off-task behavior (Neitzel, 2008). (EBP – *Functional Behavior Analysis*)
> - If the student is bothered by the sound of the pencil on paper and desk, ask him to place a workbook under his papers to lessen the sound.
> - Consider the use of headphones or earplugs to reduce auditory stimuli.
> - Consider alternate seating for the student. Options include lying on the floor, sitting in a beanbag chair or rocking chair, standing and writing at the teacher's lectern, or sitting on an air cushion or "wiggle seat." These options may assist with sensory regulation, as well as help meet the student's positioning and posture needs.

> ### Motor:
>
> Visual motor and visual perceptual difficulties are most apparent during writing tasks. Warning signs that a student might have visual perceptual/motor challenges include: difficulty grasping a pencil, difficulty forming letters correctly, difficulty keeping letters on a line, and difficulty leaving adequate space between letters and words.
>
> If you suspect a student might be having visual motor or visual perceptual difficulties, try some of the following. Start as early as possible; old habits are tough to break.
>
> - Check for the following: Can the student's feet touch the ground? Does the desk height work for functional writing? The desk should be only about two inches higher than the elbow when flexed.* The appropriate size desk and chair will not cure visual perceptual deficits, but it is amazing the positive difference in a student's quality of writing when appropriate positioning is provided.
> - Provide a pencil grip.*
> - Provide lined paper with extra space between the lines and fewer lines to focus on (http://www.therapro.com/Raised-Line-Learning-Papers-C307762.aspx).
> - Teach the student to use a spacing tool between words (see Appendix F). Younger students may benefit from a visual "spaceman," such as a tongue depressor or a clothespin. When teaching this skill, model the use of the spacer in your own writing, leave extra additional space between the words to visually model spacing between words. Older students may benefit from using the space bar on the keyboard. The authors have found that many students begin to get into the routine of typing a word, then tapping the space bar. We have also seen carryover from keyboard to paper, with spacing increasing when the student is printing by hand after using the space bar on the keyboard.

Motor (cont.):

- Use a slanted writing surface such as a three-inch, three-ring binder* turned sideways. This may be just enough of a change in positioning to assist visual perceptual skills and positioning of the writing hand.

- Reduce or eliminate far-point copying* (from overhead or chalkboard). Consider providing a close-point copy* at the student's desk that the student then has to transfer to his paper.

- Allow the student to dictate his thoughts and ideas to a peer or an adult. The peer mentor or adult can write down the ideas and the student can later copy and expand his thoughts. This allows the student to focus on one task at a time – first, composing his ideas while someone else does the writing, and second, writing the words. The use of selected classmates trained as peer tutors can be an easy and effective way to increase on-task behavior as well as encourage social interaction (Maheady, Harper, & Mallette, 2001). (EBP – *Peer-Mediated Instruction and Intervention*)

- Allow the student to use a keyboard or a portable word processor (see Appendix H).

Organization:

- If you want to measure what the student knows (as opposed to how he writes), let him use a tape recorder/voice recorder.

- For older students with good reading skills and good articulation, try speech recognition software,* in which the student speaks into a microphone and the computer types what he says. Caution! This software requires at least a fourth-grade reading level (or someone has to read the tutorial quietly to the student as he repeats it in order for the computer to develop his voice file).

- A speech recognition program* is available through Windows XP and Windows 2003. While this program is not as sophisticated as programs that are developed specifically for speech recognition, it will give you an idea of whether or not it might be an effective tool for a student.

Language:

- Try a word prediction program.* These software programs allow a child to type the first two to three letters of a word and then choose the correct spelling from a list. See Appendix H. (EBP –*Computed-Aided Instruction*)

  See also the following "Take It and Use It" worksheets: *#1 Writing Warm-Ups, #2 Big Muscle Warm-Ups, #9 Writing Warm-Ups – Sensory, #12 Writing Warm-Ups – Big-Muscle, #13 Desk Reminder – Writing Rules, #14 Hand Exercises – Ready to Write!, #15 Laser Power Letters.*

"Take It and Use It" #11
Spacer

Teacher Instructions: *Give the student a tongue depressor or clothespin to use as a spacing reminder between words.*

Name: _____ **Date:** _____

Assignment: *Remember to use your SPACER between words!*

_____

- -

_____

_____

- -

_____

_____

- -

_____

_____

- -

_____

_____

- -

_____

_____

- -

_____

"Take It and Use It" #12
Writing Warm-Ups – Big Muscle

Teacher Instruction: *For some students, the teacher/occupational therapist will need to determine which of these sensory strategies to implement, but for other students the opportunity to self-select sensory strategies will increase compliance and ownership. When the student can identify which activities help his sensory regulation, success increases. If you allow the student to self-select, do the following: At the beginning of the day, have the student select three or four from the list Self-Organizing Strategies in the Class for use that day. If choosing from the list of Work Jobs Around School or Jobs in the Classroom, the teacher will need to assist with the job chosen. Make sure all options that you offer are available (a quiet desk area, etc.). Ask the student to do his writing warm-ups before every writing assignment.*

Writing Warm-Ups – Big Muscle

Name: _____ Date: _____

Before I start my writing assignment, I will ...

Heavy Work Jobs Around School	Jobs in the Classroom	Self-Organizing Strategies in the Class
Carry breakfast crates or push breakfast cart	Use the hole punch for 5 minutes	Do deep breathing Breathe in slowly through nose, blow out through mouth 5 times
Collect recycling from classrooms	Take chairs off desks in the morning	Do 10 wall push-ups
Assist with PE equipment	Pass out papers	Do 20 jumping jacks
Push trash cans	Staple papers	Do 10 seat push-ups
Carry and deliver library books	Deliver books to another class	Chew gum while writing
Wipe off cafeteria tables	Wipe off the blackboard or dry-erase board	Listen to classical music during writing and other seat work
Run in gym/shoot baskets	Exercise with hand weights. Bend and straighten elbows 10 times; then raise weights to shoulder level 10 times	During language arts, squeeze a squeeze ball 20 times with your RIGHT hand to help your brain understand your teacher's words better. (Right-hand motor activity stimulates the left side of the brain for improved language processing.)
Deliver the attendance folder to the office	Sharpen pencils	Work in a quiet corner of the classroom
Return breakfast cart	Hold the door for everybody every time the class enters or leaves a new area	Write while sitting in a beanbag chair that is pushed into a corner of the classroom
Raise and lower a heavy therapy ball 10 times before you start writing	Carry the recess basket of balls and supplies	Wear headphones every time you write
Paper Shredding	Carry and deliver a stack of computer paper	Squeeze your fidget object for 1 minute before writing. Start writing. When you need to stop and think about your writing, squeeze it again for 1 minute. Repeat until you are finished with your writing assignment.

Writing Legibly

National Common Core State Standards for Writing:
Produce clear and coherent writing in which the development, organization, and style are appropriate to task, purpose, and audience.

Teacher Concern:
"His writing is horrible. I can't read it. The words are large and all run together. It's just not legible."

Teacher Concern:
"His writing is so small and floats above the lines. Or "He starts in the middle of the paper and then keeps writing down the side."

Why:

Students with an ASD are frequently challenged by many of the components that are needed for functional handwriting, such as sensory processing, neuromuscular tone, strength and postural control, motor skills involving the ability to cross the midline, bilateral integration* and motor planning, fine-motor coordination, visual perception, as well as cognitive abilities. Get the picture? It's hard!

Researchers have found neuroanatomical difference and abnormalities in the cerebellums of those with an ASD. These abnormalities may cause a difference in their movements and execution of motor tasks (Broun, 2009). Such differences may appear as low muscle tone and decreased strength, as well as impairment in the ability to perform skilled movements even though the individual may have the physical ability as well as desire to do so.

Directly related to this topic, a study found that graphomotor problems were significantly higher for students with ASD regardless of age or IQ and that this had a serious impact on their written expression (Mayes & Calhoun, 2003). Another study compared the written expression of 16 students with Asperger Syndrome (AS) with that of students without disabilities. Students with AS demonstrated decreased legibility, complexity, and number of words used during handwriting tasks (Myles et al., 2003). Additional support was found in a study that reviewed the school records of 40 students with AS. These students consistently struggled with various aspects of writing tasks, including organization and abstract concepts (Church, Alisanski, & Amanullah, 2000).

Finally, a research study conducted at the Kennedy Krieger Institute (Bastian, Fuentes, & Mostofsky, 2010) measured form, spacing, size, legibility, and alignment. Students who had ASD scored poorer than those who did not have ASD. The researchers studied perceptual reasoning, or the ability to reason through problems with nonverbal material. Those who scored poorly on the test of perceptual reasoning also had poor handwriting scores. The study also suggested that many children with ASD continue to have difficulty with handwriting into their teenage years.

Teaching Strategies:

Sensory:

Does your student appear disengaged and distracted by the visual and auditory distracters around him? If so, try to …

- Set up an area that can be used as a quiet "office" space for the student. (EBP – *Structured Work Systems*)
- Place a writing desk against a blank wall, away from the commotion of the classroom to help eliminate some of the competing input.
- Offer headphones or earplugs to reduce auditory stimuli.

Does your student tend to slump over his desk, rest his head on his hand? If so, try to …

- Encourage the student to perform wake-up activities before writing. All of these can be enjoyed by the entire class, and they can be extremely beneficial for the student with ASD. They include the following:
  - Run in place
  - Perform windmill movements, moving arms from side to side
  - Perform seat push-ups
  - Perform hand warm-up exercises
  - Sit on an air cushion (see Appendix I), a rolled piece of bubble wrap,* or a rocking chair cushion
  - Chew gum! We have found that it is a very easy quick fix for focus and regulation (see also Appendix J)

Motor:

Does the student have a strong motor memory for correct letter formation? If needed …

- For the younger student learning to form letters, instruction should include adult modeling of letter formation.
- The visual and verbal cues for letter formation should be consistently used by all involved.
- Students need practice repeated with the instructor providing feedback right away.
- There are many printing programs available. A particular favorite of the authors is Handwriting Without Tears (www.hwtears.com) (see Appendix E).
- Create a short video clip of forming the letter correctly. The student watches and practices the letter. See also Appendix D. (EBP – *Video Modeling*)

Does your student display a poor pencil grasp? If so …

- A poor functional pencil grasp* can make writing a nightmare by causing the student to use more energy while attempting to print letters and taking away from the actual content of what the student is trying to write. This further impacts the quantity and the quality of the assignment.

Motor (cont.):

- *If the student is printing too small,* check to see if he is holding his pencil too close to the tip of the lead of the pencil. Fingers fatigue and make it difficult to pinch in this position. If so, a small visual/tactile cue may help. For example, wrap a small rubber band or piece of masking tape on the pencil away from the lead to help the student to see where his fingers and thumb should be positioned on the pencil.

- *If the student's writing is too large,* check to see if he is using "big muscles" to form letters instead of smaller muscles intended for writing. He may be having difficulty with a traditional grip – using his thumb on the pencil. Instead, the pencil may be resting between his index finger and thumb.

If this is the case, try to …

1. Have the student practice just holding the pencil correctly (not yet on paper), drawing shapes or letters in the air.

2. Then have the student practice making some circles or lines. Do not pressure him for accuracy.

3. Then have the student practice printing his name. You may need to stay at this pace for a while, encouraging him to hold the pencil correctly each time he prints his name.

4. Try practicing with writing tools that fit the size of the young student's hand. Try pieces of crayon or chalk. Use primary crayons, pencils, golf pencils,* or markers. Older students with mechanical difficulties may be supported through the use of a pencil grip.* Habits tend to begin early with pencil positioning. The earlier the intervention the better. Ideally, by kindergarten, proper positioning should be taught.

5. Allow daily opportunity to practice at a large vertical chalkboard or dry-erase board to develop the "skill side" of the hand (these are the muscles needed for printing).

6. Use adaptive commercial pencil grips* when attempting to position the student's fingers correctly on the pencil. Try using them for short periods each day. This allows the student to get the feeling of the correct way to hold the pencil but without getting frustrated or discouraged.

7. If the student holds his pencil straight up, it tends to cause more tension in the fingers because it makes the pencil difficult to keep holding while printing in that position. Try using a large rubber band or a ponytail holder around the pencil for finger positioning. Put the rubber band on your student's wrist. Then loop another rubber band to the first. Pull the loop part over the end of the pencil near the eraser.

8. Try using a three-inch three-ring binder turned horizontally. Place the student's paper on the binder, thereby providing a slanted writing surface. It may assist with the student's hand positioning and pencil grasp as well as provide a better visual position for writing.

Motor (cont.):

- *Stabilize the paper.* If the student is not stabilizing his paper with the nondominant hand while writing, try:

  1. Wall push-ups
  2. Rubbing hands together
  3. Windmill movement exercises (swing arms from side to side across the midline of the body)
  4. Standing, raise one knee and touch the knee to the opposite elbow, then alternate movement 10 times
  5. For short periods have the student stand and hold the paper against a wall while writing. He will need to use his other hand to stabilize the paper or it will fall to the floor.
  6. Provide a visual cue that represents "Hold my paper still with my helper hand."

- For the student who starts printing in the middle of the paper and down the side of the Paper, provide a green marker line vertically down the left side of the paper. Form a red vertical line down the right side of the paper. Then explain and visually show the student that green is for start and red is for stop.

   Additional visual motor strategies are offered in Appendices D, E, F.

Technology:

Research supports (e.g., Rubel, 1999), and our experience has also found, that typically developing students during second grade (7- to 8-years-olds) have mastered the skill of correctly writing letters, including proper stroke, direction, and size. Typically, reversals of letters no longer occur. Students progress in the ability to copy from a board, and the speed of printing increases, to between 10-39 letters per minute.

Some students with an ASD do not have a problem in this area. However, for many, frustrations begin to grow, and the "I Hate to Write" emerges as the writing demands increase. Please keep in mind there are neurological abnormalities that may cause a student with an ASD to have difficulty with motor planning, which impacts the skill of being able to legibly create writing.

- Introduce keyboarding opportunities early. It is recommended that a formal keyboarding program be introduced by third or fourth grade. Schedule a few minutes of keyboard practice each day.

- Provide a peer buddy.* Keyboarding is a great tool for all. A peer buddy may assist with modeling engagement and motivation to the task. (EBP – *Peer-Mediated Instruction and Intervention*)

- Ensure that the practice time is regular, fun, and brief. That way, the student will learn that the writing process does not have to be painful!

- Refer to letter formation, keyboarding, and left-handed writing strategies in Appendices C, D, and G.

   See also the following "Take It and Use It" worksheets: *#9 Writing Warm-Ups – Sensory, #12 Writing Warm-Ups – Big Muscle.*

Teacher Instruction: *Select the writing rules you want the student to use. Copy, laminate, and tape to the student's desk as a visual cue reminder.*

 Hold my paper still with my helping hand	 Do hand exercises 5 times • **Open and close fingers** • **Squeeze hands together** • **Rub hands on legs**	 I can write or type my work	 Don't Forget to Check: • **Name** • **Complete Sentence** • **Capital letters** • **Punctuation** • **Indent new paragraph** • **Check for spelling** • **Turn in my work**
 Leave a spaghetti-thin line between the letters of a word	 Leave a meatball-size space between words	 Do 10 seat push-ups before writing	 Leave a finger space between words

"Take It and Use It" #14
Hand Exercises – Ready to Write!

Teacher Instructions: *Have the entire class do two or three of these exercises before each writing assignment to assist with waking up and preparing the upper body for the writing process.*

Hand and Upper-Body Exercises for Writing

1. Open fingers wide; then squeeze tight 10-15 times.

2. Place hands flat on desk, thumbs and pointer tips facing each other (creating a triangle), bend elbows, bring nose into triangle created between hands, then up, 10-15 times.

3. Raise arms above head, criss-cross straight arms 10 times; then put bottom arm over top hand and do 10 more.

4. Position arms at side, palms up, and then criss-cross in front of body

5. Bend elbows with palms up, shrug shoulders towards ears, release, 10-15 times.

6. Position elbows bent, fisted hands in front of shoulders, extend arms in a throwing motion, 10-15 times.

7. Position arms in front of you, elbows slightly bent, four fingers tight next to each other, thumbs open, then both hands towards thumbs at wrist, turn and return to midline position, 10-15 times.

8. Position hands holding opposite elbows, lift in a single motion over the head, return to waist, and repeat, 10-15 times.

9. Hold fingers next to ears; touch thumb to each finger (i.e., pointer, middle, ring, pinkie) and back again, 10-15 times.

10. With arms raised straight out in front of the body, make an X with thumbs, palms facing out, make small circles 10 times to the right, then 10 times to the left.

11. Seated on chair, place hands on the seat of the chair and raise bottom off the seat using upper-body strength. Repeat 10 times.

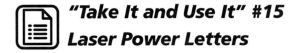

"Take It and Use It" #15
Laser Power Letters

Laser Power Letters

This activity is fun for the entire class. Students practice letter formation while their brains receive positive kinesthetic feedback.

Teacher Directions:

1. With a dark marker, write several large letters on the chalkboard or easel paper. Put a large dot on each letter where correct formation begins.

2. Tell the students they are going to "air write" some laser power letters.

3. Tell the students to pick up their pencils, grip them correctly for writing, and get ready to air write.

4. Move to the back of the classroom, dim the lights, and point a laser pointer at the starting dot of the letter on the chalkboard. Tell the students to point their pencils at the dot.

5. Beginning at the starting dot, use the laser to trace the letter slowly, verbalizing your actions as you go. Have students air write along with you.

6. After you have led the exercise, let a student be the laser power letters leader. Students love using a laser pointer.

Understanding or "Hearing" Directions

National Common Core State Standard for Speaking and Listening:
Confirm understanding of a text read aloud or information presented orally or through other media by asking and answering questions about key details and requesting clarification if something is not understood.

 Teacher Concern:
"Even when he seems to be paying attention, he doesn't seem to 'hear' my directions. Sometimes he does the first part of the assignment and then thinks he is finished. Sometimes his answers don't make any sense at all."

 Why:
Almost everybody with ASD has trouble processing oral language (Weismer, Lord, & Esler, 2010). Temple Grandin, a brilliant scientist with ASD, describes this difficulty, "I still have difficulty with long strings of verbal information. If verbal directions contain more than three steps, I have to write them down" (Grandin, 2000). If this verbal, highly educated woman has difficulty following verbal directions, imagine the difficulty our students might have!

Students with ASD often, either consciously or unconsciously, try to hide this difficulty from teachers. If you ask a student if he understands the directions, he almost always answers, "YES!" because "yes" is the answer that usually makes adults happy. The student may "look" as though he is listening, but instead he may be watching the way your mouth looks or the shine of an earring. Tuning in to what is important and tuning out extraneous sounds in the environment is frequently a challenge for students with an ASD.

Because students with ASD have so much trouble following oral directions, it is important to use visual supports to help them understand assignments and other directions. Effective visual supports answer the following questions:

Visual Support

1. What am I to do?
2. How many am I to do?
3. How will I know when I am finished?
4. What am I to do next?

 **Teaching Strategies:**

Sensory:

Before giving directions, make sure the student's sensory system is "ready to listen." The following simple strategies increase the probability that the student is ready and, therefore, will "hear" what you say.

- Listen carefully to your classroom environment. Sounds that are easy for us to ignore (like a vent blower, hallway activities, wiggly seatmate, pencil sharpener, etc.) can be deafening to a student with ASD. Position the student's seat away from any of these auditory distractions.
- Do an experiment: Try a morning with no fluorescent lights. See if this increases your student's ability to follow directions. We have had several students tell us that the lights "scream at them," making it hard to hear the teacher.
- Try tying a piece of stretchy exercise band* around the two front desk legs. This allows the student to move his lower legs/feet on and against the stretchy band for sensory regulation.
- Tell the entire class to stand up, place palms on desk, and press down hard 10 times. Then announce that you are going to give IMPORTANT directions.
- Stand near the student when you give the directions. If he does not appear to be focused on you, discreetly tap his desk. When his attention shifts to you, THEN give the directions.
- Say the student's name and wait until he looks at you. THEN give the directions.

Language:

For beginning writers: Use a First/Then* visual support. After you have given the oral instructions, break the assignment into two parts. USING AS FEW WORDS AS POSSIBLE, write what the student is to do first in the box on the left. Write what he is to do second in the box on the right. (EBP – *Structured Work Systems*)

For more advanced writers: Break your directions into three to five small chunks.* Using a visual support, write exactly what you want the student to do, USING AS FEW WORDS AS POSSIBLE. Make your instructions concrete and literal. It often helps to number the steps. Also, add a column for due date.

Organization:

Use a simple visual support with the entire class. After you give oral directions, write a simplified version of the directions on a chart at the front of the classroom. Use the rubric detailed above: 1. **What am I to do? 2. How many am I to do? 3. How will I know when I am finished? 4. What am I to do next?** (EBP – *Structured Work Systems*)

Technology:

Low-tech strategy:

- Use a dry-erase board to create a quick, simple First/Then* visual support.

High-tech strategy:

- Use a simple voice output device* such as a *Go Talk* (gotalk.com) or *Talk Pad* (www.rehabengineer.com). Record your verbal instructions in numbered steps. The student presses a number, and the device tells the student what to do. (EBP – *Speech-Generating Devices [SGD]*). While use of an SGD usually focuses on increasing a student's ability to communicate, these tools can also be used to address academic skills (Schlosser & Blischak 2001).

- Try a talking word processor program* such as *Write: Out Loud* (www.donjohnston.com). You can type your instructions directly on the student's worksheet. Whenever possible, give the instructions in step-by-step format, with examples. This allows the student to relisten to your instructions as he works. If desired, the student can wear headphones to help filter out background noise as well as to eliminate distractions from other students. (EBP – *Computer-Aided Instruction*)

- Also see the following "Take It and Use It" worksheets: *#1 Writing Warm-Ups, #2 Big-Muscle Warm-Ups, #9 Writing Warm-Ups – Sensory, #12 Writing Warm-Ups – Big Muscle, #31 Storyline.*

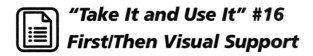

"Take It and Use It" #16
First/Then Visual Support

Teacher Instructions: *Write what the student is to do FIRST on the left. Write what the student is to do THEN on the left. Use as few words as possible. Place this visual support on the student's desk.*

Name: _____ **Date:** _____

First	Then

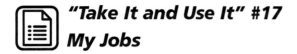

"Take It and Use It" #17
My Jobs

Teacher Instructions: *Reduce the number of words in your directions. Using as few words as possible, write the steps of the assignment on the chart below. Add a due date at the bottom.*

Name: _____ **Date:** _____

Assignment: *Do all the jobs on the list. Check "Done" when each job is finished. All the jobs must be done by the due date at the bottom of the assignment sheet.*

	My Jobs	Done
1		
2		
3		
4		
5		

Due Date: _____

Misunderstanding Directions

National Common Core State Standards for Language:
Demonstrate understanding of figurative language, word relationships and nuances in word meanings.

 Teacher Concern:
"He seems to be listening, but sometimes he completely misunderstands the assignment."

Why:
It is easy to overestimate how well students with ASD understand language. Many, especially those with Asperger Syndrome, speak very fluently and have excellent vocabulary skills, which often leads teachers to believe that the student's understanding of language is as well developed as his use of language. But this is not necessarily the case (Williams & Minshew, 2010).

Many individuals with ASD have great difficulty understanding abstract constructs like figurative language and metaphors and often interpret multiple-meaning words literally (Fein, 2011; Vicker, 2004). This may result in responses that seem perfectly logical to the student but are far different from what the teacher intended. For example:

Teacher direction: *"For tomorrow's assignment, write down what you will be doing your science project on."*

Student's written response: *"I will do my project on poster board."*

Additionally, it is often more difficult for individuals with ASD to process language when they are in a large-group setting. The student may go into survival mode by shutting down, tuning out, and engaging in off-task behavior. The task of listening to the teacher's words as he works to filter out the sensory stimuli in the room is hard. He may not be fully tuned in to the teacher's voice and may miss important parts of the instructions (Klin, 1991).

 **Teaching Strategies:**

Sensory:

Make sure you have the student's attention BEFORE you give the directions. Say the student's name or discreetly tap on his desk. When you are sure you have his attention, give advance warning before you present the main point.

- Consider seating the student at the point of instruction. This may mean that the student has several assigned seating areas in the classroom, each positioned so that he will be very near the teacher during instruction. With this arrangement, the teacher is better able to monitor whether or not the student is paying attention and give a discreet cue when he is not.
- Back up your words with a visual cue (pictures). (EBP – *Visual Supports*)
- Ask the student to deliver a quick message, get a drink of water, or take a quick stretch break before instruction. Watch for physical signs of "tuning out," such as staring into space or playing with objects on his desk.
- Watch to see if the student is stimming (repetitively flipping a pencil or other object, hyperfocusing on something in the room). If so, he probably won't hear your instructions. Discreetly tap his paper or pat him on the shoulder to get his attention before you give the directions. (EBP – *Prompting*)
- Provide a fidget* object to assist the student with self-regulation. For example, rubbing a piece of Velcro stuck under his desk or squeezing a small soft ball may decrease anxiety and increase his ability to tune into the instruction.

Language:

- Give clear, specific directions. Try to avoid similes or metaphors, unless you are prepared to explain them.
- Rephrase directions if necessary.
- Check the student's work to make sure he has understood your intent. When he does understand what is expected of him, he will be much more willing to start his writing assignments, because his stress and anxiety levels will drop noticeably.
- Visually chunk down* each part of the assignment. Break the assignment into small, concrete steps. Give the student a written example or starter phrase for each step.

    See also the following "Take It Use It" worksheets: *#1 Writing Warm-Ups, #2 Big-Muscle Warm-Ups, #9 Writing Warm-Ups – Sensory, #10 Brain Gym®, #12 Writing Warm-Ups – Big Muscle, #16 First/Then Visual Support, #17 My Jobs, #31 Storyline.*

"Take It and Use It" #18
What We Say ... What They Hear

Teacher Instruction: *Check for understanding. Look at what your student is writing to en-sure that he understood your directions. Share this "Take It and Use It" worksheet with other staff members as a reminder that students with ASD often misunderstand the directions.*

What We Say ... What They Hear

1. **"Do you understand?"**
   The teacher means: Do you understand the material I just presented?
   The student with ASD hears: Are you paying attention?
   More effective: Tell me what I said, using your own words.

2. **"This is important."**
   The teacher means: This will probably be on the test.
   The student with ASD hears: This is important to my teacher but not necessarily to me.
   More effective: Write this down. It will be on the test.

3. **"You need to ..."**
   The teacher means: I expect you to do this. If you don't, your grade will be affected.
   The student with ASD hears: The teacher thinks this is important to me, but it really isn't.
   More effective: Do this, or you will get a bad grade.

4. **"Are there any questions?"**
   The teacher means: Tell me what you do not understand.
   The student with ASD hears: The teacher is finished talking.
   More effective: Tell me what I said, using your own words.

5. **"Cut it out."**
   The teacher means: Stop doing what you are doing.
   The student with ASD hears: Am I supposed to cut something? Do I need scissors?
   More effective: Stop flipping your pencil.

6. **"I want everyone's eyes on me."**
   The teacher means: Look at me, and listen carefully to what I am saying.
   The student with ASD hears: Look at the teacher (no need to listen).
   More effective: Everyone look at me. Now listen carefully.

Spelling Words

National Common Core State Standards for Writing:
Produce clear and coherent writing in which the development, organization, and style are appropriate to task, purpose, and audience.

Teacher Concern:
"He has a lot of difficulty with spelling. He does fairly well on spelling tests, but he doesn't carry the correct spelling over to other writing tasks."

Why:
Brain researchers (Just & Minshew, 2004) have found that people with ASD remember letters in the part of the brain that ordinarily processes shapes. In contrast, people who do not have ASD tend to remember letters in the areas of the brain that primarily process language. Just and Minshew's study also revealed that the various areas of the brain of a person with ASD do not communicate with each other very efficiently.

The ramifications of these findings on spelling are significant. For example, children with ASD may be able to memorize quite easily the shapes of isolated words, including the spelling patterns. However, when asked to incorporate that spelling pattern into a longer writing task, which involves increased language and motor skills, their brains have difficulty coordinating that "shape-seeing" skill with all the language and motor requirements of writing (Just & Minshew, 2004).

 **Teaching Strategies:**

Sensory:

Use a multisensory approach* to teach spelling. For example, pair traditional methods of phonics instruction, such as systematic phonics,* with American Sign Language Manual Alphabet. It is easy to learn, and may be downloaded free of charge from http://www.lifeprint.com/asl101/topics/wallpaper1.htm. Write the spelling word on the board, spell it aloud, and manually spell it using finger spelling. Have the students finger spell along with you. (Students usually learn the signs more quickly than the teacher!) Every time you use the spelling word throughout the day, finger spell it. Encourage students to finger spell along with you. For fun, hold silent spelling bees, using finger spelling.

Additional Spelling Strategies:

Cloze Spelling Approach (Kanza, 2003):

- The student copies spelling words onto index cards.
- The teacher provides two sets of spelling word cards. One set of cards has the spelling words on it with blank spaces for the vowels in each word; on the second set of cards, blanks are left for the consonants.
  1. Student looks at a word on the card and studies the letters and their order.
  2. Student looks at a word on the card with blanks where vowels go and fills in the blanks. Student is shown the word on a card with blanks for consonants.
  3. Student writes the entire word.

Reverse Chaining by Syllable (Jones, 1998):

This technique is for more difficult, longer words.

- The teacher starts out modeling all of the following directions for the first word throughout the drill; then the student practices the drill.
- Teacher says the word and then writes it on a sheet of paper. Say each letter (be enthusiastic and expressive!):
  o S-E-P-A-R-A-T-E
- Teacher skips a line and says and writes the word again – minus the last syllable. Say the last syllable and spell it out loud, but don't write it. The student spells the word aloud with the teacher.

  o S-E-P-A-_____
- Teacher skips another line and writes only the first few letters of the word but continues to say all the spelling out loud. The student continues to spell aloud with the teacher. Teacher skips to another line, writes nothing, but spells the word aloud with the student.
- Teacher goes back to the top. The student reads the word and then spells it out loud.
- Teacher folds the page over so the student can't see the whole word. The student says the word, spells it, and adds the last syllable.
- Teacher folds the page back again. The student says the word, spells it, and adds the last two syllables.

Sensory (cont.):

- The student continues until he has spelled the whole word. The student is instructed to "GO BACK AND CHECK – make sure you didn't leave out any letters."
  - o should
  - o shoul__
  - o shou__ __
  - o sho __ __ __
  - o sh__ __ __ __
  - o s __ __ __ __ __
  - o __ __ __ __ __ __

Motor:

This is one more layer of writing, in addition to organization, language, and sensory processing. The quality of printing frequently continues to decline as motor challenges negatively impact the struggling speller. If the student is struggling with proper letter formation and also attempting to spell out the words, his writing tends to become more frustrating and less legible.

- For the younger student, provide a copy of the words from his word wall* in his personal binder. This can be a listing of commonly used vocabulary words and sight words. This allows him to find the word at close point and copy the spelling without getting frustrated.

- Consider allowing the student to dictate his sentence to you. He can help sound out and spell the words in the sentence, but when he is dictating, he does not have to perform the additional component of trying to write at the same time. If appropriate, he can then copy the sentence you have written. He will just be working on letter formation in isolation.

Technology:

- Reduce the motor and mental demands of spelling by allowing the student to use a word prediction program.* *CoWriter* (www.donjohnston.com) is an example of a program that allows flexible spelling support. The teacher can set the program to offer full word choices or word prediction options. With word prediction programs, the student types the first one to three letters of a word. A drop-down menu containing several word choices appears. The student clicks on the desired word, and the word sinks into the student's sentence without the need for additional keystrokes. These programs also read the words aloud, so the student can hear the choices. (EBP – *Computer-Aided Instruction*)

- Incorporate video modeling. Try a 2-minute instructional video of using the word prediction software* from www.donjohnston.com or by creating a short clip yourself. (EBP – *Video Modeling*)

  If a word prediction program is not available, make use of the spell check in Microsoft Word. As the student types, the red squiggle lines appear under any misspelled words. The student can then right click for the correct spelling.

- If a student's spelling is extremely poor, consider a voice recognition* software (www.dragon-dictate.com). Several programs are available. With these programs, the student speaks into a microphone, and the computer transcribes the words into text. It is recommended that the staff assess the student's ability for successful speech recognition writing. To benefit, students must be able to verbalize their thoughts and ideas into sentences. Such a program is most responsive to students who can speak audibly and are able to express thoughts and sentences orally.

  A text-to-speech program* is also built in to Microsoft Word XP. The program works best with a microphone and completion of a voice training module that is included in the program.

Organizing Words into Sentences

National Common Core Academic Standards for Writing:
Produce, expand, and rearrange complete simple and compound sentences.

 Teacher Concern:
"He can't organize his words into a logical sentence."

 Why:
Students with ASD often have trouble perceiving words as separate units (Amaral, Dawson, & Geschwind, 2011). To many, a sentence sounds like one long, continuous word. Brain scans reveal that the brains of individuals with ASD have fewer neural connections between the various language processing areas (Just et al., 2004). Therefore, while the student may have a good understanding of each of the words in a sentence, when the words are blended together into the flow of language, his brain doesn't always process the words as separate units. Consequently, the meaning of the sentence may be lost. A teacher or computer program can help the student learn to manipulate words as individual "chunks."* By adding this auditory/visual support, the brain of a person with ASD is better able to perceive the words as separate units and then organize words into meaningful sentences.

Teaching Strategies:

Language:

- Use a literacy software program such as *Clicker* (http://www.cricksoft.com/us/home.aspx) to help students learn to perceive words as separate units. Such a program allows the student to click on a word or phrase, hear it read aloud, and paste it into a sentence or paragraph. The computer can then read his sentence aloud. This multisensory approach to writing allows the student to see and hear words as separate units. It also eliminates the fine-motor requirements of writing, often resulting in increased output. (EBP – *Computer-Aided Instruction*)

Organization:

- Use your fingers as a visual organizer. Have the student tell you a sentence using the keyword. Repeat his sentence slowly, holding up a finger for each word. Keep holding your fingers up and ask the student how many words you said. Repeat the sentence again as you hold up a finger for each word. This repetition reinforces the number of words and word order. Ask the student again to tell you how many words you said. Then ask him to write those (6) words.

Motor:

- *For the student whose motor skills are challenging*: After the student has told you the 6 words of his sentence, use a yellow highlighter and draw six lines, appropriate to the length of the words on his paper. This will visually cue the student for letter/word placement and also support printing skills.   Reduce the motor requirement of writing by using a word prediction program* like *Co:Writer* (donjohnston.com), *Word Q* (http://www.goqsoftware.com), or *Scan and Read Pro* (http://www.readingmadeez.com/products/scanreadpro.html). These programs allow a student to type the first three or fewer letters of a word and then select the correct word from a drop-down menu. The computer reads the word out loud so the student can hear what he has written. Besides reducing the motor requirement, the program allows the student to hear each word as he selects it, so he knows immediately if the word is the one he wanted. But even better, the student only needs to make a few keystrokes to produce the word he wants, thus enabling faster task completion, less frustration, and better sentences.

Technology:

Try a literacy software program like *Clicker* (http://www.cricksoft.com/us/default.asp). It offers a computer program called "Find Out and Write About." This software provides technology support for organizing words into sentences. Students write by clicking on a word or phrase. The software speaks the word aloud as it pastes it into a text box. (EBP – *Computer-Aided Instruction*)

Sensory:

Remember the student is trying to hold on to the sentence he has developed (working memory) and then produce it in some form of writing. Before starting the writing process:

- Reduce auditory and visual distractions.
- Wake up writing muscles with hand and finger exercises. See also the "Take It and Use It" worksheet *#1 Writing Warm-Ups*.
- If appropriate, have the student sit on an air cushion (see Appendix I) or bubble wrap.* This may provide subtle movement and added input for alertness and concentration. Even just rolling up a jacket and sitting it on the chair vertically can give the student some extra movement as it is not a totally even surface.
- Allow the student to chew a piece of gum.
- Provide headphones for computer work. This allows the student to listen closely to the word choices from the software programs.

    See also the following "Take It and Use It" worksheets: *#1 Writing Warm-Ups, #2 Big-Muscle Warm-Ups, #9 Writing Warm-Ups – Sensory, #10 Brain Gym®, #12 Writing Warm-Ups – Big Muscle.*

"Take It and Use It" #20
Out-of-Order Sentences

Name: _____ **Date:** _____

OUT-OF-ORDER SENTENCES

Assignment: *Write a sentence. First, say your sentence out loud to your teacher. Your teacher will write each of your words in a picture box. You put them back in order!*

My sentence in order:

_____

Writing Complete Sentences

National Common Core State Standards for Speaking and Listening:
Produce complete sentences when appropriate to task and situation in order to provide requested detail or clarification.

 Teacher Concern:
"He writes in sentence fragments. His sentences don't make sense."

 Why:
ASD affects the language centers of the brain. For that reason, most individuals with ASD struggle with creative thought, auditory memory organization, and language processing (Minshew & Goldstein, 2001). This has obvious ramifications in the classroom and related to writing. For example, when we say, "Make up a sentence with this word," we are really asking the student to:

1. Think of a sentence (creative thought)
2. Remember it long enough to get it all on paper (auditory memory)
3. Write it (organization and fine motor)
4. Read/revise it (language processing)

To teach students to write in complete sentences, we may need to break down the task.

 Teaching Strategies:

Language:

- *For nonwriters*: Say, "Make up a sentence with the word 'dog.'" Repeat the child's sentence, modeling and correcting it if necessary. Have the student repeat your sentence. As he repeats the sentence, write the words on a strip of paper. Read the sentence together with the student. Cut the strip into separate words and mix them up. Have the student put the words back in order. Then have him glue the words on his paper. (Student is building skills in creative thought and organization. Teacher is supporting auditory memory, fine motor, and language processing.)

- *For beginning writers*: Have the student dictate a sentence to teacher. Repeat the sentence aloud, correcting and modeling if necessary. Write words on a strip of paper. Have the student cut the strip into separate words and glue the words in order on his paper. After the student has organized his words into a sentence, ask him to copy the sentence on a line immediately below the glued words. (Student is building skills in creative thought, organization, and fine motor. Teacher is supporting auditory memory and language processing.)

Language (cont.):

For more advanced writers:

- Have the student write a sentence alone. Read the sentence exactly as it is written and ask the student if it makes sense. Often this will be enough help for him to correct his sentence, if necessary.

- If the student doesn't catch his errors, ask him a leading question and model the sentence for him. For example, if he writes, "*The dog run house*" but does not hear any errors when he reads his sentence aloud, ask, "*Where did the dog run?*" Often when the student responds, he will add the words he has omitted in his writing. If the student responds, "*to the house,*" say, "*Good – to the house. The dog runs to the house. Now you say it.*" The student is building skills in creative thought, organization, auditory memory, fine motor, and editing. (EBP –*Prompting*)

Motor/Technology:

- Allow the student to type sentences on the computer. Reducing the fine-motor requirement often improves student output.

- Teach the student to use spell check and grammar check. These tools are available in almost all software programs.

- Use a talking word processor program that can read the student's sentences back to him. See if he can hear and correct the errors in his own sentences.

- Use a word prediction software program* such as *Co:Writer* (www.donjohnston.com). It provides visual and auditory word choices to assist him with expanding his sentence formation. *Co:Writer* even provides topic dictionary choices. Rich vocabulary words can be displayed in the corner of the computer screen to assist the student with his sentence-building skills. (EBP – *Computer-Aided Instruction*)

- Two other great software programs are *Writing With Symbols* (www.witingwithsymbols.com) and *Pix Writer* (www.pixwriter.com). In *Writing With Symbols*, a picture can appear each time the student types a word. *Pix Writer* is a picture-assisted writing program in which the student sees the pictures and receives more visual feedback to assist with building his sentence. Both of these programs can be very motivating to the struggling writer.

  See also the following "Take It and Use It" worksheets: *#1 Writing Warm-Ups, #2 Big-Muscle Warm-Ups, #9 Writing Warm-Ups – Sensory, #12 Writing Warm-Ups – Big Muscle, #27 What Do I Do?, #28 Address Sensory Needs = Write More! #29 Story Framework With Word Bank, #31 Storyline.*

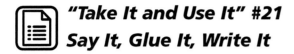 **"Take It and Use It" #21**
Say It, Glue It, Write It

WRITING COMPLETE SENTENCES

Name: _____ **Date:** _____

Assignment: ***Make up a sentence with each of your spelling words.*** *Tell your teacher your sentence. Your teacher will write it down for you. Cut out the sentence with scissors and glue it to your paper. Then use your pencil and copy the sentence.*

SPELLING WORD	GLUE YOUR SENTENCE HERE _____ COPY YOUR SENTENCE HERE
SPELLING WORD	GLUE _____ COPY
SPELLING WORD	GLUE _____ COPY
SPELLING WORD	GLUE _____ COPY
SPELLING WORD	GLUE _____ COPY

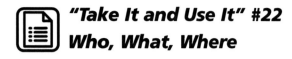

"Take It and Use It" #22
Who, What, Where

WRITING COMPLETE SENTENCES – WHO, WHAT, WHERE

Name: _____ **Date:** _____

Assignment: *Write a sentence about each picture. Tell **WHO** is in the picture, **WHAT** the person is doing, and **WHERE** the person is. The first one is done for you.*

spirit of america /
Shutterstock.com

President Obama	**is standing**	**by a flag.**
(Who)	(What)	(Where)

(Who)	(What)	(Where)

(Who)	(What)	(Where)

(Who)	(What)	(Where)

(Who)	(What)	(Where)

Organizing a Paragraph

National Common Core State Standards for Writing:
Write informative/explanatory texts to examine a topic and convey ideas and information clearly.

 Teacher Concern:
"He can't organize his thoughts into an organized paragraph."

 Why:
Students with ASD have difficulty with organization at all levels (Adreon & Willis, 2011). In day-to-day tasks, they tend to lose assignments, and their lockers often look like they erupted. Even very high-functioning individuals with ASD struggle with organizing the mundane tasks of everyday life.

The act of writing requires organization at many levels even before the student begins to tackle the assignment of writing a paragraph. Most of us are not conscious of each step that is performed when writing, but for those with an ASD each step of the process may require deliberate effort. First he must organize the tools needed for writing. Next he must organize his ideas into a cohesive thought. Then he must organize sounds into words and words into sentences. All of this must be done before the student can begin to address the thorny task of organizing a paragraph. It is a daunting task for an individual with ASD (Adreon & Willis, 2011).

Teaching Strategies:

Sensory:

If the student is having difficulty blocking out whispering in the class, subtle sounds of pencil on paper, and other noises that others are able to filter out, it further complicates the task of learning how to organize his thoughts. Visual sensitivities can also greatly impact concentration. For example, students have shared that the fluorescent lighting in a classroom feels like experiencing a strobe light. We have heard "the lights hurt my head." If the student cannot get his body to calm and feel grounded, it will further intensify the difficulty of organizing his written work.

- Encourage heavy work activities* for sensory regulation. This refers to pushing/pulling/lifting/carrying types of jobs. Even if it is just "pushing the wall away" by performing wall push-ups, it may help to clear his thoughts for better writing. Please refer to the "Take It and Use It" worksheet #2 *Big-Muscle Warm-Ups*.
- Check the lights. Do they need to be on? Try turning off half, provide table lamps, or use natural lighting.
- Provide ear buds or earphones with music. This can help regulate the student while writing.
- Place a workbook under the writing paper to muffle the scratchy sound.

Sensory (cont.):

- Provide a writing "office area" for concentration: cubicle or cozy corner.
- Offer positioning choices: on the floor, standing at desk/chair, kneeling with one leg in the chair, beanbag, working in quiet hallway or resource room. (EBP – *Antecedent-Based Intervention*)

Language:

- Break the task into two parts – content and organization. Give the student several blank strips of paper. Have him write one complete sentence about the topic on each strip. Tell him that neatness doesn't matter. (He'll like that!) When he has several sentence strips filled, help him arrange them into a logical order. THEN have him copy his sentences into a paragraph.

Organization:

Help the student create a simple story web. Draw an oval and put #1 in it. Ask him what the paragraph is about. Write one key word in the oval. Draw a line coming out from the oval and put a #2 on it. Ask the student to tell you something about the topic. Write one key word on line #2. Draw another line coming out from the oval and put #3 on it. Ask the student to tell you something else about the paragraph. Write one key word on line #3. Continue this pattern until the student has a web with five or six lines/key words. He now can start with #1 and write an organized paragraph with one sentence for each key word. (Hint: Have him put a period after each key word on the web. This reinforces the idea that each line represents a complete sentence.)

Motor:

- Think about what you are trying to teach the student. Writing the sentences may be so frustrating for students with ASD that they give up before they ever reach the organization stage. If this is the case, have someone else type the sentences. Then have the student cut and paste (either by hand or using a keyboard) the sentences into an organized paragraph.

Technology:

- Consider using technology to help the student organize his ideas. *Kidspiration* (www.kidspiration.com) for kindergarten through fourth to fifth grade is an outstanding graphic organizer* and writing aid. It provides a visual library where students may add a picture to their graphic web as they type their key words or short sentences into the organizer. With only a click on an icon, all of the graphic organizer work is put into an outline form, organized for the student to then add further information. It even talks back to the student and reads his work to him! (EBP – *Computer-Aided Instruction*)

- Help older students organize their thoughts with *Inspiration* (www.inspiration.com). This is an amazing graphic organizer* that is very engaging for all students. This program provides mature graphic organizing that is computer based. Both are marvelous programs to assist students in growing skills and independence.

- If a software program is not feasible, try clicking in Microsoft Word/Insert Tab/SmartArt. Here you will have choices of tools that can assist with graphic organizing.

See also the following "Take It and Use It" worksheets: #7 Story Frame, #8 Pictures With Numbers, #9 Writing Warm-Ups - Sensory, #10 Brain Gym®, #12 Writing Warm-Ups – Big Muscle.

 **"Take It and Use It" #23**
Keyword Story Web

Teacher Instructions: *First, have the student tell you the topic of the paragraph, then you write a keyword at #1. Second, ask the student to tell you one thing about the topic, then you write a keyword at #2. Continue until there is one keyword on each line. Each line represents a complete sentence. Using the numbers as prompts, ask the student to "read" his paragraph to you. Model and shape as needed in this verbal retelling. On a separate piece of paper, have the student write the paragraph, using the numbered lines and keywords as a visual support.*

Name: _____ **Date:** _____

Assignment:

1. With your teacher's help, write one keyword on each line of this story web. Start with #1.

2. Using the keywords as reminders, start with #1 and tell your teacher what you are going to write in your paragraph.

3. On a separate piece of paper, write your paragraph. Start with #1. Then write a sentence for #2. Write a sentence for each number on your story web. When you are finished, you will have at least seven sentences in your paragraph!

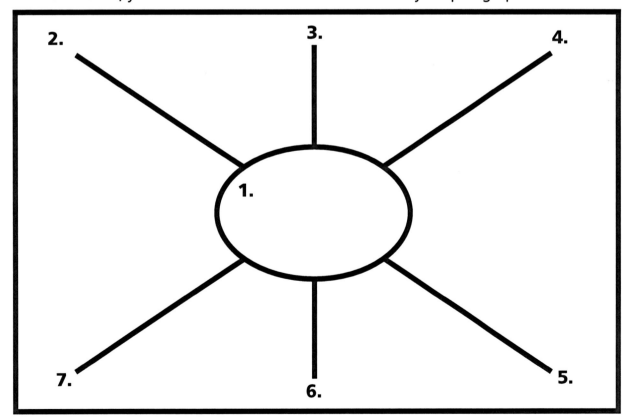

"Take It and Use It" #24
Film Strip Paragraph

Name: _____ **Date:** _____

Assignment: *You are writing ideas for a movie script about _____.*
Write one idea on each piece of movie film. Make sure each idea is in the form of a complete sentence. You can put them in order later.

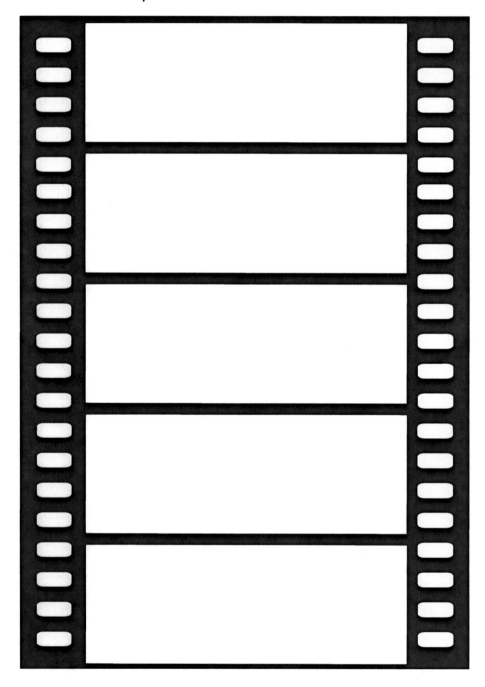

Writing Paragraphs That Flow

National Common Core State Standards for Writing:
Use linking words and phrases (e.g., because, therefore, since, for example) to connect opinion and reasons or to connect ideas within categories of information (e.g., also, another, and, more, but).

 Teacher Concern:
"There is no flow to his paragraphs. They either look like one long run-on sentence, or they look like a laundry list of facts."

 Why:
People with ASD usually are not sequential thinkers (Perry, 2009). That is, their brains process language as isolated chunks of information rather than as thoughts that flow from one idea to another. This is reflected in their writing. Because they don't tend to see ideas as being related to each other, students with ASD often omit linking words and phrases.

 Teaching Strategies:

Language and Organization:

For beginning writers:

- Provide a framework in which the student only has to write in the keywords. Guide the student's writing by providing transition words, sentence starters, and punctuation.

- Ask the student to "Build a Burger." In this simple writing strategy, the student writes his topic sentence on the top bun, his concluding sentence on the bottom bun, and three details in between. Many variations of this simple graphic organizer* are available commercially. The authors' personal version is included here as a "Take It and Use It" worksheet.

- Have the student read the story aloud that he has written so he can hear the flow of the language.

- Later, have him copy the entire paragraph on the computer or on a blank sheet of paper. Then have him read the story aloud again. The multisensory* input of doing, seeing, and hearing the flow of his story with the transition words will help him generalize the skill.

For more advanced writers:

- Provide a framework but with less scaffolding.* Include transition words in the scaffold.

- For longer written assignments, break the task down into discrete chunks. Ask the student to turn in each section of the assignment as he completes it. When all the sections are complete, have the student read the entire text aloud to an adult. This will allow him to hear the flow of the language. It will also allow the adult to prompt when additional transition words are needed for clarification or emphasis.

- Allow the first draft to be a "sloppy copy." As long as the student can read what he has written, don't worry about neatness. When all revisions and edits have been completed on the "sloppy copy," THEN give the student a clean sheet of paper and ask him to copy his work into a neat version. Only ask him to write three or four sentences at a time. Praise his work, have him do a short sensory regulation activity (see Appendix I), then ask him to write three or more sentences. By chunking the writing requirement in this fashion, the student will be less inclined to feel overwhelmed by the writing task.

Technology:

- Allow the student to type sentences on the computer. Reducing the fine-motor requirement often greatly improves student output.

- Teach the student to use spell check and grammar check. These tools are available in most software programs.

- Use a talking word processor program that can read the student's sentences back to him. See if he can hear and correct the errors in his sentences. A software program such as *Write Out Loud* (www.donjohnston.com) provides auditory feedback and allows the student to hear each word, sentence, or paragraph that he has written. (EBP – *Computer-Aided Instruction*)

- Try other programs. For example, *Kidspiration* (www.kidspiration.com) helps students create a paragraph through the use of pictures and a visual outline. The teacher can choose from many types of graphic organizers,* depending on the student's needs and the particular writing assignment. The teacher can add question/answer prompts to help the student develop his picture outline. Then with a click of the button, the program will send the information into a traditional outline form on lined computer paper. *Draft: Builder* (www. draftbuilder.com) is another option. The student can brainstorm his "laundry list" and then click and drag it in the correct order. Once he can see his "working memory," he may be able to make his paragraphs flow.

"Take It and Use It" #25
Write Your Keywords

Teacher Instruction: *Use this sample story or develop a similar one on a different topic.*

Name: _____ **Date:** _____

Assignment: *Write a paragraph about your best friend. Provide sentence starters and punctuation. Include as many words as needed for the student to be able to write a paragraph with appropriate sequence and order.*

My Best Friend _____

_____ is my best friend. I see him at _____

_____. We first met _____

_____. I knew he would be a good friend

because _____ .

_____ and I like to _____

_____. One time we _____

_____. That was so _____

_____! The best thing about _____

is _____ .

I like having _____

for my best friend.

"Take It and Use It" #26
Build a Burger Paragraph

Name: _____ **Date:** _____

Assignment:
1. Write your topic sentence on the top bun.
2. Write one detail on the cheese.
3. Write one detail on the meat.
4. Write one detail on the lettuce.
5. Write your concluding sentence on the bun.

Build a Burger

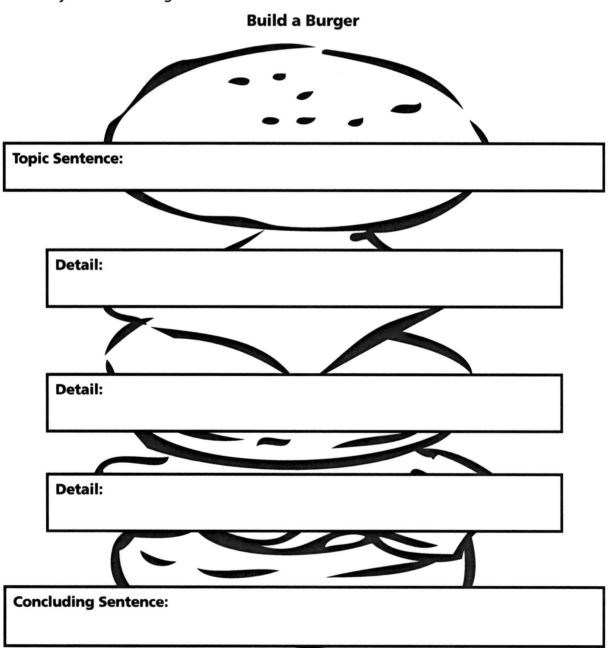

Topic Sentence:

Detail:

Detail:

Detail:

Concluding Sentence:

Writing the Bare Minimum

National Common Core State Standards for Writing:
Develop the topic with relevant, well-chosen facts, definitions, concrete details, quotations, or other information and examples.

 Teacher Concern:
"His sentences are so brief! He doesn't develop his ideas."

 Why:
Several factors may contribute to a student's tendency to write the bare minimum. First, students with ASD tend to think very concretely and literally (Paxton & Estay, 2007). In their minds, facts are facts. Emotional overlay, multiple meanings of words, and supporting arguments seem confusing and superfluous. They need some form of scaffolding* to help them know when to embellish ideas and add descriptions. Without such scaffolding, they tend to just state the facts (Paxton & Estay).

Second, organizational skills are difficult for students with ASD (Winner, 2005). For example, they have difficulty sequencing thoughts into a logical format. They also have a strong need for structure. They need to know detailed information about "What do I do, how much do I do, and what do I do when I am finished."

Third, the profound effect that sensory overload can have on behavior has been well documented (Donnelan, Hill, & Leary, 2010). Sensory overload often occurs during writing tasks. When the sights, sounds, and smells of the classroom are compounded by the sensory stimuli of holding a pencil and rubbing the hand across a piece of paper, the student's sensory system may feel bombarded. The result of sensory overload is often a need to escape. Thus, the student may write the bare minimum, just to be finished with the task.

Finally, eye-hand coordination and fine-motor control are often areas of weakness for students with ASD (Provost, Lopez, & Heimerl, 2007). Holding a pencil and knowing how much pressure to exert may cause physical pain for some students. Difficulties with eye-hand coordination often make letter formation challenging. Writing can be a physically exhausting task!

Teaching Strategies:

Language:

- Use a graphic organizer* to help the student know exactly how many supporting sentences to write in each paragraph.

- Provide a word bank of adjectives. Tell the student he must use a different adjective in each supporting sentence.

- Help the student to create a visual picture. What does he see in his "picture"? Visually ask how big, what color, how does it feel, what do you smell? Jot down these words to add to his word bank.

- When possible, provide a picture for the student or allow him to draw a picture. Ask specific questions related to the picture. (EBP – *Visual Supports*)

Organization:

- Provide the student with a visual support that lists: *What do I do, how much do I do, and what do I do when I am finished.* Include precise information such as the number of sentences the student must write, and where the student should put the paper when he is finished. (EBP –*Structured Work Systems*). Be sure to include a positive reinforcement after the task has been completed. Research shows that one of the easiest and most effective ways to increase on-task behavior is to reinforce it (Pelios, MacDuff, & Axelrod, 2003). (EBP – *Reinforcement*)

Sensory:

- Spend 5 minutes on Brain Gym® (braingym.org) or similar exercises to support brain activation, alertness, and internal organization. Also refer to "Take It and Use It" worksheets *#9 Writing Warm-Ups – Sensory* and *# 10 Writing Warm-Ups – Big Muscle.*

- Have student stand at a dry-erase board to brainstorm ideas.

- Provide a pacing area. Remember: Movement may facilitate language.

- Toss a 12" ball back and forth. This may get the student's brain and body more engaged.

Motor:

- Experiment with various writing tools. A fine-tip marker or gel pen provides different sensory input. These may reduce negative auditory input.

- Try a scented pencil.*

- Have the student try a pencil grip.* If the student has a poor grasp, it may discourage lengthier writing attempts. A pencil grip may decrease strain/fatigue and promote proper positioning for functional writing. Some students enjoy the tactile input of a good pencil grip while others just need a visual cue to put their fingers in the correct area and not too close to the tip of a pencil. A small piece of tape or a rubber band can provide a quick fix by helping the student know exactly where to put his fingers on the pencil.

- Provide lined paper with extra space between the lines. Sentences may be brief when perceptual skills are challenged and it's just too much work to place words on a line.

- Let the student use a tape recorder/voice recorder.

- Allow the student to dictate his thoughts and ideas to an adult or to a carefully selected peer tutor. The adult/peer tutor can write down the ideas, which the student can then copy or keyboard onto paper. By reducing the initial motor demand, students often automatically verbally express more. And the added benefit of having a peer do some of the student's writing can place a very positive spin on this social interaction. (EBP – *Peer-Mediated Instruction and Intervention*)

- Spend a few minutes each day working on fine-motor skills. Your occupational therapist can recommend appropriate hand/finger exercises. (Refer to Appendix D.)

- Since any kind of writing probably won't be a preferred activity for the student, make sure that this practice period be *short, fun, and positive.* Always praise, and end the activity with a reinforcer. (EBP – *Reinforcement*)

  See also the following "Take It and Use It" worksheets: #9 *Writing Warm-Ups – Sensory,* #10 *Brain Gym®,* #12 *Writing Warm-Ups – Big Muscle.*

"Take It and Use It" #27
What Do I Do?

Teacher Instructions: *Laminate this visual support and attach it to the top of the student's work area. With a dry-erase marker, write brief, but very specific instructions for the student. You may prefer to make multiple copies of this visual support and use it to increase independent seatwork.*

Example:

Under WHAT DO I DO, write the basic assignment; for example, *"write a paragraph about _____."*

Under HOW MUCH DO I DO, write *"six sentences, with capitals and punctuation. Each sentence must include one adjective."*

Under WHAT DO I DO WHEN I AM FINISHED, write *"give finished paragraph to teacher."*

WHAT DO I DO?

start!

HOW MUCH DO I HAVE TO DO?

WHAT DO I DO WHEN I AM FINISHED?

"Take It and Use It" #28
Address Sensory Needs = Write More!

Teacher Instructions: *Increase your student's time on task by addressing sensory needs before and during writing assignments. Try some of the following ideas.*

- Allow the student to do his writing task in a quiet area, with reduced visual and auditory stimuli. A study carrel placed against the wall may help. If the student continues to struggle, allow him to wear headphones during writing tasks.

- Bring out the gum. We have found that many students have increased their time on task when chewing a piece of (sugarless) gum. See also Appendix J.

- If the student is working at the computer, check to see if the background on the screen may be more engaging to him if light blue.

- Check desk/chair* seating. It may feel uncomfortable, tiring, and unstable for the student. Allow him to have a choice: try sitting on an air cushion, comfy cushion, beanbag chair, or even bubble wrap folded on the seat.

- Consider using a large therapy ball for the student who appears "tired" and "un-motivated." He may be struggling from poor sensory regulation. Let the student sit and bounce on the ball for a couple of minutes and then get to work.

- Try turning the student's chair backwards; he will be straddling his legs on each side. The back of the chair may provide front support and calming pressure to the front of the student while writing.

- Turn on music. Music that provides a consistent beat may support rhythm and timing, which is frequently challenging for our students. Music may assist language, attention, and focus

- Ask the student to place his paper on top of a workbook. This will decrease the scratchy noise of pencil against paper.

- Provide a wake-up call and upper-body strengthener for the muscles needed for writing. Perform upper-body exercises before writing. Seat push-ups and hand exercises are quick and easy.

- Remember that many students verbalize their thoughts more when they are moving as opposed to sitting down. Allow them to stand and dictate their ideas or even pace in a visually identified area.

- Remember to praise, praise, and praise for each positive step!

Writing With Description

National Common Core State Standards for Writing:
Write narratives to develop real or imagined experiences or events using effective technique, descriptive details, and clear event sequences.

 Teacher Concern:
"He writes the bare minimum. He uses VERY little description."

 Why:
Students with ASD are usually very concrete thinkers. Their brains tend to look at the world in very literal terms (Perry, 2009). Therefore, thinking and writing about objects, people, places, or events in descriptive and imaginary ways is like learning a new language. It is often so frustrating to the student that he gives up.

 Teaching Strategies:

Language:

- *For beginning writers:* Provide a story frame. Build a word bank with the student. Include three choices for each description. Write the words in the word bank. Help the student circle the descriptive words that best describe his chosen person/event. Have the student copy the selected descriptive words into the framework. If the student is unable/unwilling to write the words, he can draw lines from the selected vocabulary to the appropriate blank in the story.

- Provide a picture or pictures of the writing topic or story. (EBP – *Visual Supports*)

- *For intermediate writers:* Provide a word bank of adjectives/descriptive words at the student's desk. (Many students with ASD have trouble visually tracking from the chalkboard/wall to their paper.) Visually tell the student how many sentences his paragraph must have. Tell the student that each sentence must contain at least one descriptive word.

Sensory:

The student who is sensory regulated, calm, and internally organized is more apt to learn the skills needed to expand his descriptive writing.

- Set him up for success. Adapt the environment to meet his sensory challenges. In order to help the student learn how to manage his regulation needs, let him choose from a short list of options. For example, let him choose his seating option such as on the floor or at his desk; his writing tool: computer or paper/pencil; and his writing location: in the class or in the hall. Other sensory regulation strategies are included in Appendix I. (EBP – *Antecedent-Based Intervention*)

- Play detective: What is your student's behavior trying to tell you from a sensory component? Does he look draggy, unmotivated, is his head resting on his hand? Wake up his system! What is available in your setting? A long hallway for a fast walk? A mini-trampoline for 2 minutes of jumping? A jump rope that could be used in a resource room? (EBP – *Functional Behavior Assessment*)

  Wake the student up by asking him to turn his head side to side, up and down, ear to shoulder five times in each direction.

- Help your student if he is having difficulty calming down, settling, or sitting still.

  Apply deep pressure touch through his shoulders or seat him in a large beanbag chair with the padding around him, or if you are in a resource room, ask him to perform 10 slow log rolls forward on the floor and 10 log rolls slowly coming back. Lying on the floor with arms above head or across chest, have him slowly perform full body rolling.

  See also the following "Take It and Use It" worksheets: *#3 Picture Prompts – Make It Concrete!, #4 Visual Timeline, #7 Story Frame, #8 Pictures With Numbers, #9 Writing Warm-Ups – Sensory, #10 Brain Gym®, #12 Writing Warm-Ups – Big Muscle, #23 Keyword Story Web, #24 Film Strip Paragraph, #27 What Do I Do?, #28 Address Sensory Needs = Write More!*

"Take It and Use It" #29
Story Framework With Word Bank

Teacher Instruction: *Use this sample, or develop a similar one on a different topic. Write a story framework on the left side of the paper. Develop a word bank with choices on the right side of the paper.*

SAMPLE USING STORY FRAMEWORK PLUS WORD BANK

Name: _____ **Date:** _____

Assignment: *Write a descriptive story about your favorite family member.*

_____MY GRANDMA_____	**WORD BANK**
This is a story about my _____. My grandma is	Grandma
	Nice
very _____. She is _____ and	Loving
	Sweet
	Short
	Tall
	Fat
	Skinny
_____. My grandma has _____ hair.	Black
	White
	Brown
	Blonde
When I hug her, she feels _____. She smells like	Soft
	Scratchy
	Squishy
	Cookies
_____. My grandma makes me feel	Perfume
	Shampoo
	Happy
_____.	Sad
	Loved

Writing and Editing

National Common Core State Standards for Writing:
With guidance and support from adults and peers, focus on a topic and strengthen writing as needed by revising and editing.

 Teacher Concern:
"When I ask him to edit and revise his work, he just looks at it, but he doesn't make any changes."

Why:
People with ASD are <u>one-track thinkers</u>. Generally, they can do only one task at a time (Freedman, 2010). Many are so literal that after the rough draft, they view the writing as done: "I wrote!" However, that's barely the beginning. The task of editing/revising requires the student to:

1. Check to see if what he wrote makes sense.
2. Check for capitalization errors.
3. Check for punctuation errors.
4. Check for spelling errors.
5. Check for grammar errors.
6. Check for other errors that the teacher says are important!

To a person with ASD, "editing" is not one task. It is six tasks! The student will be more successful if he is only asked to edit one thing at a time. A visual checklist is much more effective than verbal reminders (Luiselli, 2008).

Teaching Strategies:

- Teach the student to edit one skill at a time. After the student has written his paragraph, have him proofread it, using the editing checklist. Fold or cover part of the paper so the child only checks one editing task at a time.
- After each editing task, immediately praise the student for a task well done. Be specific in your praise. Celebrate the fact that he edited and corrected all punctuation, or all the capital letters. Emphasize how quickly and well he did that one task of editing. Then encourage him to move on to the next editing task on the sheet. Be prepared to provide a positive behavior support after every group of edits. Mix up your verbal praise with more tangible reinforcers, such as allowing him to draw for 2 minutes. Keep the reinforcers short to encourage the student to complete the entire task. Start with editing a short assignment. By going through the editing checklist with one short paragraph, the student experiences success much faster. (EBP – *Reinforcement*)
- With lower functioning students or those who have difficulty recognizing what has to be edited, modify the requirement for independent work. Still focusing on only one editing task at a time, do one or two sentences with the student, then ask him to do the rest on his own. Repeat this support for each new editing task.

Sensory:

- Consider taking a 5-minute sensory break before starting the first edit, and again when the student has finished half of the editing tasks.
- If a walk is feasible, direct the student to deliver a quick message.
- Remember that a lot of postural control, muscle strength, and motor control is needed during writing. Restretch shoulders, arms, and hands.
- Hand out a peppermint candy or a piece of gum to assist with refocusing on the editing. See also Appendix J.

Motor/Technology:

(The computer is great for teaching a student to edit and revise his work. Most word processing programs have spell check, grammar check, and text-to-speech built into the software. These tools are immediately accessible, very visual, and "ASD friendly.") (EBP – *Computer-Aided Instruction*)

- Use the following four-step process to help the student edit using technology:
  1. Have the student write his paragraph with pencil-paper. Then type the student's text, exactly as the student has written it, on the computer. Don't clean up anything. Include all spelling, grammar, punctuation, and spacing errors.
  2. Have the student look for words that have red lines. These are spelling errors. Tell the student to right click and choose correct spelling.
  3. Have the student look for words that have green lines. These are grammar or punctuation errors. Tell the student to right click and choose correct grammar and punctuation.
  4. Have the student point to each word as he slowly reads his text aloud to see if it makes sense.

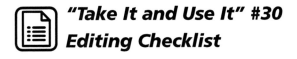 **"Take It and Use It" #30**
Editing Checklist

Name: _____ **Date:** _____

Assignment: *Edit your writing, one step at a time. Fold or cover this paper so only one number shows at a time. Check "I did it" when you finish each task.*

Editing Checklist

1	*Check for capital letters.* • First words in sentences • Proper nouns – people, places, dates, etc.	I did it. _____
2	*Check for punctuation (. , ? !,").* • At the end of sentences • After abbreviations like Mr. and Dr.	I did it. _____
3	*Check for spelling.* • If you aren't sure how something is spelled, check the word wall or a dictionary.	I did it. _____
4	*Check for grammar.* • Make sure you didn't accidentally leave out little words like *a, an, the, of, as, but.*	I did it. _____
5	*Check to make sure your writing makes sense.* • Read slowly what you wrote. Touch each word as you read it. Does it make sense?	I did it. _____
6	My teacher also wants me to check:	I did it. _____

Thinking in Pictures

National Common Core State Standards for Writing:
Use a combination of drawing, dictating, and writing to narrate a single event or several loosely linked events, tell about the events in the order in which they occurred, and provide a reaction to what happened.

 Teacher Concern:
"Printed words don't seem to mean anything to him."

 Why:
Most students with ASD "read" pictures long before they learn to read words (National Autism Center, 2009). Research findings of the National Standards Project include the use of visual supports (i.e., pictures) as one of the evidence-based practices that are most important in helping students with ASD be successful in school. Further, Temple Grandin, a world-renowned scientist with ASD, wrote a book, *Thinking in Pictures* (1995), that describes this phenomenon. Dr. Grandin says, "I think in pictures. Words are like a second language to me. I translate both spoken and written words into full-color movies, complete with sound, which run like a VCR tape in my head. When somebody speaks to me, his words are instantly translated into pictures" (p. 3).

Because the brain of a person with ASD tends to process language in a visual format, traditional phonetic approaches to reading are often unsuccessful. A whole-word approach to reading and writing, supplemented by simple pictures, is generally much more effective. Adding pictures to printed text often helps students with ASD take that leap toward understanding and using printed words.

Students with ASD also have difficulty organizing and sequencing thoughts, especially in print format. They may be able to visualize a well-developed idea, but for them getting that idea on paper is a challenge similar to having to translate it into a different language. At the sentence level, words are often out of order. At the paragraph level, thoughts often don't follow each other logically. In longer writing tasks, time and sequence are often distorted. At each of these levels, simple picture cues can help the student translate the idea in his head to the printed word on the paper. Temple Grandin stated, "Every design problem I've ever solved started with my ability to visualize and see the world in pictures" (2006, p. 4).

Teaching Strategies:

Language:

- Use pictures, including photographs, line drawings, icons, pictures from a textbook, etc. Even very high-functioning students with ASD are more successful at understanding what you want them to write about if they are provided with picture cues. (EBP – *Visual Supports*)

Organization:

- For longer written assignments, provide a timeline or storyline* as a visual support. If the assignment has a component of sequence and chronology, it is best to call it a timeline. If the assignment is geared more toward creative thought, you might call it a storyline. Regardless of the title, the process of using this strategy is the same. As the student talks through his idea, draw VERY simple pictures representing his ideas along a straight line. Using probing questions, help the student flesh out his idea, placing new pictures on the line while the student speaks. As needed, discreetly arrange the pictures into a logical order during this brainstorming process. Or, after all ideas have been represented on the line, arrange them into an appropriate sequence with the student. At the end of the exercise, have the student "read" the assignment out loud. This verbal rehearsal will help him hear the logical flow of the language. Following the verbal rehearsal, the student writes the assignment using the timeline/storyline as a visual support.

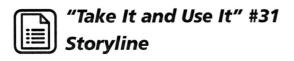

"Take It and Use It" #31
Storyline

Name: _____ **Date:** _____

FOLLOWING A STORYLINE

Assignment: *Tell your ideas to a teacher. The teacher will draw idea reminders on the storyline. When the storyline is finished, tell your teacher the story, using the idea reminders. Then use the idea reminders to write your story. Use another piece of paper if you need more room.*

_____

   1.   **2.**   **3.**   **4.**   **5.**   **6.**   **7.**   **8.**

_____

_____

_____

_____

_____

_____

_____

Writing a Book Report

National Common Core State Standards for Reading:
Describe how a particular story's or drama's plot unfolds in a series of episodes as well as how the characters respond or change as the plot moves toward a resolution.

Teacher Concern:
"He only wants to read nonfiction books. Since we are currently focusing on characters, motivations, and plot, I have required the students to choose fiction books this time. He seems totally lost."

Why:
While some students with ASD enjoy the world of fantasy and imagination, many others find nonfiction much more logical and meaningful. This poses challenges when it is time for students to write a book report (Murray, 2009). The student with ASD who enjoys fantasy and fiction may be somewhat inflexible in his choices of reading material. His imaginative thoughts may be rich but rigid. They may only extend to specific characters such as Pokémon or Harry Potter. When required to read and report on fiction that stretches his imagination outside of this comfort zone, the student may have so much difficulty accepting this stretch that he is unable to keep his attention focused on character and plot. On the other hand, many individuals with ASD consider fiction boring and a waste of time. Why spend time reading about something that isn't real? These students may be excellent readers, but they often have comprehension difficulties when required to read fiction material. Comprehension difficulty is very evident when they are asked to write a report about the book. Even highly intelligent students with ASD may have difficulty relating character motivations and plot lines from fiction material (Iland, 2011).

 Teaching Strategies:

Language:

Think about your goal for the lesson. If the student can accomplish that goal by reading and reporting on a book within his range of preferred reading, let him use that book. If you think it is necessary to broaden his horizon, be prepared to add support when it is time for him to write his book report. If he only likes to read nonfiction, you may need to help with many of the figurative language aspects of the book. Idioms, which are frequently used in fiction texts, are often a total mystery to a student with ASD.

- For some students, the use of a mnemonic helps organize and improve their writing. The POW and WWWWhat-2 How 2 strategies, explained below, may increase the number of words the student uses, inclusion of story elements, and quality of overall story writing (Sansosti, Powell-Smith, & Cowan, 2010).

POW stands for:

P-Pick my ideas

O-Organize my notes

W-Write and say more.

WWWWhat-2 How-2 refers to the parts of the story and stands for

1. Who are the main characters?
2. When does the story take place?
3. Where does the story take place?
4. What do the main characters want to do?
5. What happens when the main characters try to do it?
6. How does the story end? How do the main characters feel? Paired with a picture prompt.

Organization:

Many students are overwhelmed with all the steps involved in writing a book report.

- Break it down. Provide the student with a template with only one aspect of the book report requirements on each page. On each page, include a BRIEF explanation of exactly what and how much the student must write. Instead of having the student keep the entire book report template until it is finished, have him turn in each page as soon as it is completed. Include a "due date" for each page.
- Provide a bank of choices for abstract aspects of the book, such as character motivation, cause/effect relationships, and predictions.

Sensory:

Frequently the classroom consists of too much talk and not enough visuals for students with ASD, who are visual learners. The verbal bombardment of this type of classroom makes multistep assignments such as book reports overwhelming and, as a result, many students give up and don't write at all.

- Encourage the student to be his own advocate. Ask him, "Do you feel you will work better at the corner computer in class or do you need the quiet of the resource room?" (EBP – Antecedent-Based Intervention)
- Suggest that the student take a quick hall walk, do 20 push-ups, and then chew a piece of gum. The 20 minutes of quality work time is well worth the 5-10 minutes needed for a movement break versus 30 minutes of struggle and nonproductivity.

Motor:

Though his printing may be poor, the student may find that he can print faster than he can hunt and peck on a keyboard. Pick your battles. If the student prefers to print, allow him to do his rough draft with paper and pencil. Each day have him type and save three of his sentences into a final draft on the computer. Make the typing requirement concrete and short enough so that the student feels successful in the task.

- Scan or type the book report template into a computer program. Save the template in a large font. This will cause the student's responses to default to this same large font. Tell the student that he must use the same font as the template. This reduces his tendency to spend computer time playing with various sizes and colors of print.

- Allow the student to dictate to you first. Then he can copy the writing, thus working only on making his work look legible without trying to do it all at once.

- Take turns printing or typing with the student.

- Set up a schedule for three times a week to progress with keyboarding tutorial skills. (EBP –*Computer-Aided Instruction*)

Technology:

- Try *Draft:Builder* (wwwldonjohnston.com.) Most struggling writers spend less than 1 minute on planning their writing. Providing technology support makes it visually organizing and engaging to students with an ASD.

- *Kidspiration* (www.kidspriration.com) is also highly recommended. The graphic web is engaging to students with a visual library that supports ideas. After the student has created his web, then with a click, the outline is put into a draft format. He doesn't have to rewrite it all over again!!!

"Take It and Use It" #32
Check for Understanding – Idioms

Teacher Instruction: *Check for understanding. Share this "Take It and Use It" with other staff members as a reminder that students with ASD often misunderstand figurative language.*

Name: _____ **Date:** _____

Assignment: *Keep this list of idioms in your writing folder. Tell your teacher if you find an idiom in your book.*

IDIOMS

The Idiom	What It Really Means
I take that with a grain of salt.	I don't really believe that.
There's something fishy here.	Something is wrong.
I need you to be all ears today.	Listen VERY carefully.
Zip your lip.	Stop talking NOW.
You'll be ahead of the game.	You will have already finished some of the work.
Give your seatmate a hand.	Help the person sitting next to you.
No time like the present.	Do it now.
It's time to hit the books.	Do the work NOW.

"Take It and Use It" #33
Book Report Template

Teacher Instructions: *Make this template reflect your terminology and requirements of the assignment. Have the student keep the checklist in his binder. Assign a due date to each section of the book report, and require that each section be turned in as soon as it is completed.*

Name: _____ **Date:** _____

Assignment: *Write a book report. Keep this chart in your binder. Check DONE when you finish a section.*

BOOK REPORT	Name on paper DONE	This part is DONE	Turned In DONE
TITLE PAGE			
CHARACTERS			
SETTING			
PLOT			
ENDING			
WHAT I THINK ABOUT THE BOOK			
FINAL COPY			

Name: _____ **Date:** _____

The Title of My Book Is: _____
The Author Is: _____
My Name: _____   **My Teacher's Name:** _____   **Today's Date:** _____

Give this page to my teacher on: _____

Name: _____ **Date:** _____

Main Characters

Most of this story takes place: _____

boy   girl   animal

One interesting thing about this setting is: _____

_____

Other characters in this book are: _____

_____

_____

Give this page to my teacher on: _____

Name: _____ Date: _____

Setting

Most of this story takes place: _____

in a house

in a forest

---

on a playground at school in a jungle **?** Somewhere else. Write the setting.

One interesting thing about this setting is: _____

_____

Give this page to my teacher on: _____

Name: _____ **Date:** _____

Plot

At the beginning of the book, the main character:_____

_____

(Write what the main character is doing when the story starts.)

What happens next? _____

_____

Then what happens? _____

_____

Give this page to my teacher on: _____

Name: _____ **Date:** _____

The Ending

The End

At the end of the story: _____

(Write how the story ends.)

_____

_____

What I Think

I think this book was: _____

good   bad   OK   exciting   boring

Give this page to my teacher on: _____

Writing a Lab Report

National Common Core State Standards for Writing – Science/Technical:
Conduct short research projects to answer a question (including a self-generated question), drawing on several sources and generating additional related, focused questions that allow for multiple avenues of exploration.

 Teacher Concern:
"He likes doing the science projects, but he hates writing the lab reports."

 Why:
Students with high-functioning ASD often thrive in the hands-on, multi-sensory world of science (Secor, n.d.). These students tend to be precise and detail oriented and gravitate to the factual nature of the scientific experiment. Thus, many students with ASD who sit silently in language arts and history classes become excited, active participants in the science lab.

Unfortunately, this excitement usually doesn't carry over to the task of writing the lab report. For students, the "doing" of the scientific method comes naturally. The "writing" of the scientific method does not. Even the most gifted students with ASD are more successful with this task if the steps are broken down, visual supports are provided, and very specific timelines/due dates are established.

Teaching Strategies:

Language:
- Rephrase the steps of the scientific method in very basic terms.
- Personalize the directions.
- Use as few words as possible to make expectations very clear.
- Use simple pictures as visual reminders of what the student is addressing in a particular step of the lab report.
- Provide visual schedule so the student can view how much he has to do to complete the assignment. (EBP – *Visual Supports*)

Organization:

- Break the writing requirements of the lab report down into distinct chunks.
- Assign one step of the scientific method at a time.
- Use a separate piece of paper for each step of the scientific method.
- Allow the student to focus on just that one aspect of the method until he has completed that step.
- Require the student to turn in each segment of the lab report as soon as it is completed. (EBP –*Structured Work Systems*)

Sensory:

The student may be very involved in the science experiment. However, as he tries to focus on writing the report (generally a less favored activity), consider the smells, visual distractions, and sounds within a science lab. If the student is having trouble starting the lab report, it might be due to sensory overload.

- Allow the student to go to another area or take a movement break prior to writing.
- Try muffling the noisy metal legs of the stools by placing cut tennis balls on the bottom of each leg. (EBP – *Antecedent-Based Intervention*)

Motor:

- Consider pairing the student with a partner. The student with ASD may dictate to the science partner, who acts as the writer. (EBP – *Peer-Mediated Intervention and Instruction*)

  If you give the student a worksheet to complete, yellow highlight the areas where the student is to write his answers. This will draw his attention to all the areas on the worksheet that need an answer. For students who tend to write too large, tell them that all their letters must be written on the yellow lines. (If you use this strategy, make sure your yellow highlights are large enough to accommodate all that the student might want to say!)

Technology:

- Consider the use of a portable word processor such as a DANA (www.renlearn.com/neo). A portable word processor may increase the student's motivation to do the "write-up." The portability of the device makes it a great tool to use during lab reports. A peer buddy* could still taking turns typing the information.
- Consider the use of a talking word processor. The template for the science report could be provided. The student can hear and see the question and then directly type his answer on the template. See also Appendix H. (EBP – *Computer-Aided Instruction*)

"Take It and Use It" #34
Lab Report/Scientific Method Template

Name: _____ **Date:** _____

Assignment: *Write a lab report using the scientific method. Keep this chart in your binder. Check DONE when you finish a section.*

LAB REPORT – SCIENTIFIC METHOD	Name on paper DONE	This part is DONE	Turned In DONE
PURPOSE			
RESEARCH			
MATERIALS			
HYPOTHESIS			
EXPERIMENT			
ANALYSIS			
CONCLUSION			

Name: _____ **Date:** _____

The Scientific Method

Purpose
What am I trying to learn?

The purpose of this project is to find out:_____

_____

_____

_____

_____

_____

This page is due on _____

Name: _____ **Date:** _____

The Scientific Method

Research

What have I learned about this subject from books and the internet?

One thing I learned about this subject: _____

_____

_____

Another thing I learned about this subject: _____

_____

_____

Sources
Books, authors, and Internet sites I used for this project

_____

_____

_____

This page is due on _____

Name: _____ **Date:** _____

	The Scientific Method	

Materials

What do I need to do this project?

For this project I will need these things: _____

_____

_____

_____

_____

_____

This page is due on _____

Name: _____ **Date:** _____

The Scientific Method

Hypothesis

What do I think will happen?

I think: _____

_____

_____

_____

_____

_____

This page is due on _____

Name: _____ **Date:** _____

The Scientific Method

Experiment

Write all the steps to my experiment.

First: _____

Second: _____

Third: _____

Fourth: _____

Fifth: _____

Sixth: _____

Seventh: _____

This page is due on _____

Name: _____ **Date:** _____

The Scientific Method

Analysis

What happened? What did I see?

One thing that happened:_____

_____

Another thing that happened: _____

_____

Something else I noticed: _____

_____

Also, _____

_____

This page is due on _____

Name: _____ Date: _____

The Scientific Method

Conclusion

What did I learn? Was my hypothesis correct?

This is what I thought would happen (my hypothesis): _____

_____

This is what really happened: _____

_____

My hypothesis was: CORRECT   /   NOT CORRECT

The most important thing I learned was: _____

_____

This page is due on _____

Writing a Research Paper

National Common Core State Standards for Writing:
Conduct short as well as more sustained research projects to answer a question (including a self-generated question) or solve a problem; narrow or broaden the inquiry when appropriate; synthesize multiple sources on the subject, demonstrating understanding of the subject under investigation.

 Teacher Concern:
"The big project for this grading period is a research paper. He does bits and pieces of the work, but he either forgets to turn it in or he quits working on it altogether."

 Why:
People with ASD have trouble breaking large assignments down into smaller chunks. A psychologist might say that the student can see the "gestalt," or the whole picture, but is unable to see the parts (Bogdashina, 2005). Teachers generally provide their students with very clear outlines that describe each required step of the project. This is helpful, but the steps may have to be made more concrete for the student with ASD to ensure he truly knows what he has to do. Also, many students with ASD have severe organizational difficulties, which result in lost assignments and failure to turn in required pieces of work. When a high-stakes assignment such as a research paper is not completed and turned in, it can make the difference between a student passing or failing an entire class. At the high school level, this can ultimately affect a student's ability to graduate with a standard diploma.

 Teaching Strategies:

Language:
- Remember that one of the keys to success is to make sure the student knows the big three: *What am I supposed to do? How much do I have to do? What do I do when I am finished?* Look at your class outline for the project. Try to make it more concrete, using fewer words. Put each step of the project on a separate piece of paper. For some students, it helps to give an example that they can use as a model. At the bottom of the paper, write a due date for the individual segments. (EBP – *Structured Work Systems*)

Organization:

- Only give the student one concrete section of the project at a time. Even if the rest of the class is able to follow the outline independently, even a very high-functioning student with ASD will be more successful if the teacher tells him exactly what he is supposed to do on that particular day.

- Too often the finished parts of long assignments end up lost at the bottom of the student's locker. Even if the other students will be keeping the pieces of the project in their desks or binders, require the student with ASD to turn in each day's work as soon as it is completed.

- Set a visual timer* to assist the student in connecting with "how long" he has to stay on task. (EBP – *Structured Work Systems*)

Sensory:

Awake, alert, calm and focused. Is that how you would describe your student? If not, what can you have him do before he writes to help him initiate and attend to the task?

Some ways to help elementary students get their sensory system ready for writing:

- Have students run in place for 2 minutes before writing.

- Have students perform brain-activating exercises (10 repetitions front and back of the cross crawl from Brain Gym®; www.braingym.org).

Some ways to help secondary students get their sensory system ready for writing:

- Ask them for assistance in passing out papers.

- Ask them to make a quick trip to the library to deliver a crate of books.

- Direct students to a study carrel or quieter area with fewer visual and auditory distractions. (EBP – *Antecedent-Based Intervention*)

Motor:

For the student struggling with motor skills during a research paper, try …

- When doing research, give the student a yellow highlighter. He can highlight meaningful notes and then cut out the notes and place them on index cards to help organize his report.

- Support the student by enlarging the paper for each chunk* of the assignment.

- Use appropriately lined sheets of paper. Many students with ASD find it difficult to print in a small, confined space. Paper with fewer lines may help. The student can then attend more successfully to placing the letters near the line. If his work is legible enough for him to read, he may then attempt to write more.

Technology:

- Use a computer. When working at the computer, the student may be able to handle the entire writing process, including locating his saved work and turning it in. If each section is saved on the computer, the work will be easy to locate when it is time to turn it in.

- Software such as SOLO (donjohnston.com) provides support from start to finish.

- Remember to include time for practice with a good keyboarding tutorial. See Appendix G. (EBP – *Computer-Aided Instruction*)

"Take It and Use It" #35
Research Paper Template: Elementary

Teacher Instructions: *Make this template reflect your terminology and requirements of the assignment. Have the student keep the checklist in his binder. Assign a due date to each section of the research paper, and require that each section be turned in as soon as it is completed.*

Name: _____ **Date:** _____

Assignment: *Write a research paper. Keep this chart in your binder. Check DONE when you finish a section.*

RESEARCH PAPER	Name on paper DONE	This part is DONE	Turned In DONE
TOPIC/TITLE PAGE			
RESEARCH – BOOKS			
RESEARCH – INTERNET			
ROUGH DRAFT – INTRODUCTION			
ROUGH DRAFT – BODY			
ROUGH DRAFT – CONCLUSION			
FINAL COPY			

RESEARCH PAPER – Elementary

Your report is about: _____

Write your name here: _____

Draw a picture about your topic in this box:

Turn this page in to your teacher on: _____

Your Name: _____ **Date:** _____

Research

Find __2__ books about your topic. _____ **can help you.**

Book # 1:
Title: _____

Author: _____

Year the book was written: _____

Book # 2:
Title: _____

Author: _____

Year the book was written: _____

Turn this page in to your teacher on: _____

"Take It and Use It"
Page 3

Your Name: _____ Date: _____

Gathering Information – Books

Find two interesting things about your topic from Book #1. Then find two different things about your topic from Book #2.

Book # 1:

1. _____

_____

_____

2. _____

_____

_____

Book # 2:

1. _____

_____

_____

2. _____

_____

_____

Turn this page in to your teacher on:_____

Your Name: _____ **Date:** _____

Gathering Information – Internet

Find one interesting Internet site about your topic. You have _____ minutes to choose a site. Then write three interesting things about your topic. They must be different from the things you chose from books.

Website: _____

Three interesting things about my topic. (Must be different from what you wrote about Book #1 and Book #2.)

1. _____

_____

_____

2. _____

_____

_____

3. _____

_____

_____

Your Name: _____ Date: _____

Writing the Rough Draft – Introduction

Write the first paragraph of your report. This is a rough draft, so your teacher must be able to read it, but your writing does not need to be neat. *Your teacher will make corrections and changes to this rough draft. You will write the final copy later.*

Introduction rough draft. **Write a paragraph with three sentences. Remember to use capital letters and punctuation.**

_____

(Write a topic sentence that tells what your report is about.)

_____

_____

(Write a sentence that tells why your topic is interesting.)

_____

_____

(Write a sentence that tells the MOST important thing about your topic.)

_____

_____

Turn this page in to your teacher on: _____

Your Name: _____ **Date:** _____

Writing the Rough Draft – Body

Write the second paragraph of your report. This is a rough draft, so your teacher must be able to read it, but your writing does not have to be neat. *Your teacher will make corrections and changes to this rough draft. You will write the final copy later.*

Body rough draft. **Ask your teacher to give you your research sentences from Book #1, Book #2, and the Internet. Your teacher can help you number the sentences so they are in a good order for your report. Copy the sentences, in the right order, here. Your teacher might want you to add more sentences.**

_____

_____

_____

_____

_____

_____

_____

_____

_____

_____

Turn this page in to your teacher on: _____

Name: _____ **Date:** _____

RESEARCH PAPER – Middle School/High School

Research Question:

_____

_____

_____

Hook: *(What is interesting about this question? Tell one thing that will make your reader want to know more about this topic.)*

_____

_____

_____

Introductory Paragraph: *(Combine the research question and the hook into a paragraph. The paragraph should contain at least three sentences. This will be the Introduction of your research paper.)*

_____

_____

_____

_____

_____

WHEN THIS PAGE IS COMPLETE, TURN IT IN TO YOUR TEACHER.

"Take It and Use It"
Section 2

Name: _____ **Date:** _____

Research: (*Find three articles about your topic.*)

First article:
According to (*author's name*) _____

(*date the article was written*)_____, the most important thing about

this subject is: _____

_____

_____ .

The article states that (*list three facts from this article that give information about your topic*).
First, (*Fact 1*)_____

_____ .

Second, (*Fact 2*) _____

_____ .

The article also states that (*Fact 3*) _____

_____ .

Paragraph #2 *(Starting with the words, "According to," write a paragraph with all the information from above. Your paragraph should have at least four sentences.)*

_____

_____

_____

_____

_____

_____

_____

_____

_____

WHEN THIS PAGE IS COMPLETE, TURN IT IN TO YOUR TEACHER.

"Take It and Use It"
Section 3

Name: _____ **Date:** _____

Research: *(Find three articles about your topic.)*

Second article:
Additional information about (your topic) _____

was found in an article by *(author's name)* _____

*(date the article was written)*_____.

According to *(author's name)* _____ ,

(List three facts from this article that give information about your topic. Make sure they are different from the facts you listed from the first article).

*(Fact 1)*_____

_____ .

Another interesting fact is *(Fact 2)* _____

_____ .

The article also states that *(Fact 3)* _____

_____ .

Paragraph #3 *(Starting with the words, "Additional information," write a paragraph with all the information from above. Your paragraph should have at least four sentences.)*

_____

_____

_____

_____

_____

_____

_____

_____

_____

_____

WHEN THIS PAGE IS COMPLETE, TURN IT IN TO YOUR TEACHER.

"Take It and Use It"
Section 4

Name: _____ **Date:** _____

Research: *(Find three articles about your topic.)*

Third article:
Finally, further information about *(your topic)* _____

was found in an article by *(author's name)* _____

*(date the article was written)*_____.

According to (this *author's name*) _____ ,

(List three facts from this article that give information about your topic. Make sure they are different from the facts you listed from the other articles).

*(Fact 1)*_____

_____.

Also, *(Fact 2)*_____

_____.

The article also states that *(Fact 3)* _____

_____.

Paragraph #4 *(Starting with the word, "Finally," write a paragraph with all the information from above. Your paragraph should have at least four sentences.)*

_____

_____

_____

_____

_____

_____

_____

_____

_____

_____

_____

_____

WHEN THIS PAGE IS COMPLETE, TURN IT IN TO YOUR TEACHER.

"Take It and Use It"
Section 5

Name: _____ **Date:** _____

Summary and Conclusion:

In summary, this research paper explored (*write your research question here*) _____

_____

_____ .

This is an interesting topic because (*write why the topic is important to know about*).

_____

_____ .

(*Write the most important fact from your research here.*)_____

_____

_____ .

I believe that (*write your opinion about your research question*) _____

_____

_____ .

In conclusion, (*write a short ending sentence*) _____

_____

_____ .

Paragraph #5 *(Starting with the words, "In summary," write a paragraph with all the information from above. Your paragraph should have at least five sentences.)*

_____

_____

_____

_____

_____

_____

_____

_____

_____

_____

WHEN THIS PAGE IS COMPLETE, TURN IT IN TO YOUR TEACHER.

Writing a Letter

National Common Core State Standards for Writing:
Produce clear and coherent writing in which the development and organization are appropriate to task, purpose, and audience.

 Teacher Concern:
"He doesn't seem to understand the purpose of writing a letter. He says that the idea of talking with another person on paper is just silly."

 Why:
Three factors come into play when a student with ASD is asked to write a letter. First, there is the challenge of imagining the invisible audience. *"How can I write to somebody I can't see?"* Second, there is the challenge of perspective taking (Baron-Cohen & Swettenham, 1997). Individuals with ASD often have a hard time understanding that other people might have ideas and perspectives that are different from their own. *"Why should I write a thank you letter to Grandma? She already knows I liked the present she gave me."* Third, there is the perpetual challenge of organization. Individuals with ASD often struggle to organize their thoughts into a clear and coherent format (Winner, 2007). Formatting ideas into the conversational structure of a letter can be very difficult. *"Why should I write a letter to the principal telling him how he could improve our school? I can just give him a list of what he needs to do."*

Teaching Strategies:

Language:
- Provide pictures and some verbal rehearsal. Even with very high-functioning students, these two strategies will help them generate ideas for writing. The pictures can be fancy – downloaded from the Internet or cut from a magazine. Or they can be very simple – stick figures drawn quickly by the adult to help the student remember and organize his ideas. (EBP – *Visual Supports*)

- Regardless of the type of pictures used, before he writes anything, help the student verbally rehearse his letter. Referring to the pictures and "reading" his letter out loud before he writes it reinforces the flow of the language.

Organization:
- Provide a template for structure. Write the framework of the letter, with empty spaces where the student can fill in strategic information. The amount of leading text provided by the adult will vary, depending on the student's ability to generate his own text. Once the organizational framework is completed, the student can write his clean copy on a separate piece of paper.

Sensory:
Students with self-regulation challenges may be showing inappropriate behaviors with little motivation to write a letter. The better regulated the student is the better she may accept the task and the better her response. Ideas for regulation include …
- Having the student bounce on a large exercise ball
- Holding a brainstorming session at the dry-erase board
- Letting the student rock in a rocking chair
- Providing a fidget object*

Motor:
Students with severe motor challenges can create a letter by pasting words or pictures into a teacher-generated framework. It is important that the adult provides enough, but not too much, support in this type of activity. Encourage the student to generate the ideas as much as possible. Model and expand the student's ideas if necessary, but try to maintain the student's own thoughts. If the student has the motor skills needed to copy text, have him create a "clean copy" of his letter. (EBP – *Prompting*)

Time for the computer: For many students, keyboarding increases the success of letter writing. Clear, legible, typed words may promote more engagement in the writing process. When the student is able to clearly read what he has written, he may discover an additional thought or sentence to add to the letter.

"Take It and Use It" #37
Example – Writing a Letter Template With Visual Choices

Teacher Directions: *Provide a template for structure. On a separate piece of paper, provide a list of suggested answers. Support the options with picture cues whenever possible. If the student has extreme difficulty with paper-pencil tasks, allow the student to cut and paste from your picture/word options.*

Example:

Dear *President Obama*   ,

My name is *Kathy*   , **and I am** *8*   **years old.**

I am in the *second* **grade at** *Central Elementary School*   . **I have**

some ideas for things that might help our *country*   .

Here are my top two ideas:

Idea Number 1: *schools should have everything they need for every student, no*

matter who they are or where they live.

Idea Number 2: *everyone who wants to work should be able to find a job.*

_____

Thank you for reading my letter and thinking about my ideas.

Sincerely,

Kathy Oehler

Assignment: *Use the pictures on Page 2 to complete this letter. You may write your own words, or you may choose pictures and words from Page 2.*

Dear_____ ,

My name is _____ **, and I am** _____ **years old.**

I am in the _____ **grade at** _____ . **I have**

some ideas for things that might help our _____ .

Here are my top two ideas:

Idea Number 1: _____

_____

Idea Number 2: _____

_____

Thank you for reading my letter and thinking about my ideas.

Sincerely,

_____

Teacher Directions: *Use these picture supports to prompt writing choices.*

President Obama	Governor Daniels	Mayor Ballard	second	third
			2	3

fourth	fifth	country	state	city
4	5			

Schools should have everything they need for every student, no matter who they are or where they live.

Everyone should have a safe place to live.

Everyone should feel safe on the playground and in the cafeteria. Bullies should be punished.

Everyone who wants to work should be able to find a job.

References

Adreon, D., & Willis, H. (2011). *Teaching organizational skills.* Autism Support Network. Retrieved from http://www.autismsupportnetwork.com/news/teaching-organizational-skills

Aman, M. G., Arnold, L. E., & Armstrong, S. C. (1999). Review of serotonergic agents and perseverative behavior in patients with developmental disabilities. *Mental Retardation and Developmental Disabilities Research Reviews, 5,* 279-289.

Amaral, D., Dawson, G., & Geschwind, D. H. (2011). *Autism spectrum disorders.* New York City, NY: Oxford Press.

Assistive Technology Training Online Project (ATTO). University of Buffalo. Buffalo, NY. Funded by U.S. Department of Education's Office of Special Education and Rehabilitation Services. http://atto.buffalo.edu/

Autism research finds empirical link between multisensory integration and autism. (2010, August). Albert Einstein School of Medicine. Yeshiva University. Bronx, NY. Available ay http://www.einstein.yu.edu/news/releases/564/autism-research-finds-empirical-link-between-multisensory-integration-and-autism/

Ayres, J. (1979). *Sensory integration and the child: understanding hidden sensory challenges.* Los Angeles, CA: Western Psychological Services.

Ayres, J. (2000). *Sensory integration and the child.* Los Angeles CA: Western Psychological Service.

Baron-Cohen, S., & Swettenham, J. (1997). Theory of mind in autism: Its relationship to executive function and central coherence. In D. J. Cohen & F. R. Volkmar (Eds.), *Handbook of autism and pervasive developmental disorders* (pp. 880-893). New York, NY: Wiley & Sons.

Bastian, A., Fuentes, C., & Mostofsky, S. (2010). Handwriting problems affect children with autism into the teenage years. *Neurology, 73,* 1532-1537.

Bennett-Brown, N. (2008). *The relationship between context and sensory processing patterns in children with autism.* Ann Arbor, MI: ProQuest Information and Learning Company.

Blischak, D. M., & Schlosser, R. W. (2003). Use of technology to support independent spelling by students with autism. *Topics in Language Disorders, 23*(4), 293-304.

Bloom, B. S. (1986). Automaticity: "The hands and feet of genius." *Educational Leadership, 43*(5), 70-77.

Bogdashina, O. (2005). *Communication issues in autism and Asperger Syndrome: Do we speak the same language?* Philadelphia, PA: Jessica Kingsley Publisher.

Broun, L. (2009). Take the pencil out of the process. *Teaching Exceptional Children, 42*(1), 14-21.

Brown, N. B., & Dunn, W. (2010, May). Relationship between context and sensory processing in children with autism. *American Journal of Occupational Therapy, 64,* 474-483.

Bryan, L., & Gast, D. (2000). Teaching on-task and on-schedule behaviors to high functioning children with autism via picture activity schedules. *Journal of Autism and Developmental Disorders, 30,* 553-567.

Burman, D. (2009). *Gender differences in language abilities: evidence from brain imaging.* Retrieved from www.education.com/topic/gender-differences/

Chan, J. M., Lang, R., Rispoli, M. O., Reilly, M., Sigafoos, J., & Cole, H. (2009). Use of peer-mediated interventions in the treatment of autism spectrum disorders: A systematic review. *Research in Autism Spectrum Disorders, 3,* 876-889.

Church, C., Alisanski, S., &Amanullah, S. (2000). The social behavioral and academic experiences of children with Asperger Syndrome. *Focus on Autism and Other Developmental Disabilities, 15*(1), 2-20.

Craig, J., & Baron-Cohen, S. (1999). Creativity and imagination in autism and Asperger Syndrome. *Journal of Autism and Developmental Disorders, 29,* 319-326.

De Boer, S. R. (2009). *Successful inclusion for students with autism: Creating a complete effective inclusion program.* San Francisco, CA: John Wiley & Sons.

Dennison, P. E., & Dennison, G. E. (2010). *Brain Gym®. Teacher's edition.* Ventura, CA: Edu-Kinesthetics, Inc.

Dettmer, S., Simpson, R., Myles, B., & Ganz, J. (2000). The use of visual supports to facilitate transitions of students with autism. *Focus on Autism and Other Developmental Disabilities, 15,* 163-170.

Dodd, S. (2005). *Understanding autism.* Sydney, Australia: Elsevier.

Donnelan, A., Hill, D. A., & Leary, M. (2010). Rethinking autism: Implications of sensory and movement differences. *Disability Studies Quarterly, 3*(1). Retrieved from http://dsq-sds.org/article/view/1060/1225

Fein, D. (2011). *The neuropsychology of autism.* New York, NY: Oxford University Press.

Fleming, S. (2002). *When and how should keyboarding be taught in elementary schools?* Unpublished master's thesis, University of Northern Iowa, Cedar Falls, Iowa.

Freedman, S. (2010). *Developing college skills in autism and Asperger's Syndrome.* Philadelphia, PA: Jessica Kingsley Publisher.

Grandin, T. (1995). How people with autism think. Learning and cognition in autism. In T. Grandin, *Current issues in autism* (pp. 137-156). New York, NY: Plenum Press.

Grandin, T. (1995). *Thinking in pictures and other reports from my life with autism.* New York, NY: Bantam Doubleday Dell Publishing Group.

Grandin, T. (2000). *My experiences with visual thinking, sensory problems and communication problems.* Retrieved from http://legacy.autism.com/families/therapy/visual.htm

Grandin, T. (2006). *Thinking in pictures.* New York, NY: Vintage Books Division of Random House, Inc.

Gray, C. (2008). Foreword. In K. D. Buron & P. Wolfberg (Eds.), *Learners on the autism spectrum: Preparing highly qualified educators* (pp. 7-8). Shawnee Mission, KS: AAPC Publishing.

Greenspan, S. I., & Wieder, S. (1998). *The child with special needs: encouraging intellectual and emotional growth.* Reading, MA: Perseus Books.

Hamilton, J. (n.d.). *Writing study ties autism to motor-skill problems.* National Public Radio. Retrieved from http://www.npr.org/templates/story/story.php?storyId=120275194

Herbert, M., Ziegler, B. S., Nikos, M., Filipek, P., Kemper, T. L., Normandin, B. A. et al. (2004). Localization of white matter volume increase in autism and developmental language disorder. *Annals of Neurology, 55,* 4.

Hetzroni, O. E., & Tannous, J. (2004). Effects of a computer-based intervention program on the communicative functions of children with autism. *Journal of Autism and Developmental Disorders, 34*(2), 95-113.

Hoot, J. (1986). Keyboarding instruction in the early grades: must or mistake? *Childhood Education, 63*(2), 95-101.

Horner, R., Carr, E., Strain, P., Todd, A., & Reed, H. (2002). Problem behavior interventions for young children. *Journal of Autism and Developmental Disorders, 32*(5), 423-446.

Howard Florey Institute. (2005, October 25). Autism problems explained in new research. *Science Daily.* Retrieved from http://www.sciencedaily.com /releases/2005/10/051025074915.htm

Howell, P., Davis, S., & Williams, R. (2008). Late childhood stuttering. *Journal of Speech, Language, and Hearing Research, 51*(3), 669-687.

Hume, K., & Odom, S. (2007). Effects of an individual work system on the independent functioning of students with autism. *Journal of Autism and Developmental Disorders, 37,* 1166-1180.

Iland, E. (2011). *Drawing a blank. Improving comprehension for readers on the autism spectrum.* Shawnee Mission, KS: AAPC Publishing.

Jasmin, E., Couture, M., McKinley, P., Reid, G., Fombonne, E., & Gisel E. (2009, February). Sensori-motor and daily living skills of preschool children with autism spectrum disorders. *Journal of Autism Developmental Disorders, 39*(2), 231-241.

Jones, S. (1998). *Five guidelines for learning to spell and six ways to practice spelling.* Retrieved from http://www.resourceroom.net/readspell/guidespell.asp.

Just, M. A., Cherkassky, V. L., Kellar, T. A., & Minshew, N. J. (2004). *Cortical activation and synchronization during sentence comprehension in high-functioning autism: Evidence of under-connectivity.* Presentation at Research Showcase, Carnegie Mellon University Dietrich College of Humanities and Social Sciences. Department of Psychology. Paper 323. Pittsburgh, PA. Available at http://repository.cmu.edu/psychology/323

Just, M. A., & Minshew, N. J. (2004, November). *Brains of people with autism recall letters of the alphabet in brain areas dealing with shapes.* National Institute of Child Health and Human Development. Retrieved from http://www.nichd.nih.gov/news/releases/final_autism.cfm

Kanza, D. (2003). *Teaching children with reading difficulties.* Katoomba, NSW, Australia: Social Science Press.

Kimura, D. (2000). *Sex and cognition.* Cambridge, MA: A Bradford Book/The MIT Press.

Klin, A. (1991). Young autistic children's listening preferences in regard to speech: A possible characterization of the symptom of social withdrawal. *Journal of Autism and Developmental Disorders, 21,* 29-42.

Leekam, S. R., Nieto, C., Libby, S. J., Wing, L., & Gould, J. (2007). Describing the sensory abnormalities of children and adults with autism. *Journal of Autism and Developmental Disorders, 37,* 894-910.

Luiselli, J. K. (2008). Antecedent (preventive) intervention. In J. K. Luiselli, D. C. Russo, W. P. Christian, & S. M. Wilczynski (Eds.), *Effective practices for children with autism: Educational and behavioral support interventions that work* (pp. 393-412). New York, NY: Oxford University Press.

Maheady, L., Harper, G. F., & Mallette, B. (2001). Peer-mediated instruction and interventions and students with mild disabilities. *Remedial and Special Education, 22*(1), 4-14.

Mayes, S., & Calhoun, S. (2003). Ability profiles in children with autism: Influence of age and IQ. *Autism, 7,* 65.

Miller, L. J. (2006). *Sensational kids: Hope and help for children with sensory processing disorder (SPD).* New York, NY: G. P. Putnam's Sons.

Minshew, N., & Goldstein, G. (2001). The pattern of intact and impaired memory functions in autism. *Journal of Child Psychology and Psychiatry, 42*(8), 1095-1101.

Mirenda, P. (2003). "He's not really a reader …" Perspectives on supporting literacy development in individuals with autism. *Topics in Language Disorders, 23,* 271-282.

Mostofsky, S. H., Powell, S. K., Simmonds, D. J., Goldberg M. C., Caffo, B., & Pekar, J. J. (2009). Decreased connectivity and cerebella activity in autism during motor task performance. *Brain, 132,* 2413-2425.

Murray, N. L. (2009). *Exploring the relationship between early interventions and reading.* Ann Arbor, MI: ProQuest LLC.

Myles, B. S., Rome-Lake, M., Barnhill, G. P., Huggins, A., Hagiwara, T., & Griswold, D. (2003). Written language profile of children and youth with Asperger Syndrome: From, research to practice. *Education and Training in Developmental Disabilities, 38*(4), 362-369.

National Autism Center (NAC). (2009). *Evidence-based practice and autism in the schools.* Randolph, MA: Author. Retrieved from: http://info@nationalautismcenter.org

National Autism Center (NAC). (2009). *Findings and conclusions of the national standards project: Addressing the need for evidence-based practice guidelines for autism spectrum disorders.* Randolph, MA: Author.

National Professional Development Center on Autism Spectrum Disorders (NPDC). (2009). *What are evidence-based practices?* Retrieved from http://autismpdc.fpg.unc.edu/content/evidence-based-practices

Neitzel, J. (2008). *Implementation checklist for functional behavior assessment.* Chapel Hill, NC: The University of North Carolina, The National Professional Development Center on Autism Spectrum Disorders, Frank Porter Graham Child Development Institute.

Ory, Nathan. (2001). *Working with perfectionist anxiety.* Retrieved from http:// www.autismtoday.com.

Paxton, K., & Estay, I. (2007). *Counseling people on the autism spectrum: A practical manual.* Philadelphia, PA: Jessica Kingsley Publisher.

Pelios, L. V., MacDuff, G. S., & Axelrod, S. (2003). The effects of a treatment package in establishing independent academic work skills in children with autism. *Education and Treatment of Children, 26*(1), 1-21.

Perry, N. (2009). *Adults on the autism spectrum leave the nest achieving supported independence.* Philadelphia, PA: Jessica Kingsley Publisher.

Provost, B., Lopez, B. R., & Heimerl, S. (2007). Comparison of motor delays in young children: Autism spectrum disorder, developmental delay, and developmental concerns. *Journal of Autism and Developmental Disorders, 37*(2), 321-328.

Rubel, B. L. (1999). *Big strokes for little folks.* Chicago, IL: Psychological Corp.

Sansosti, F., Powell-Smith, K., & Cowan, R. (2010). *High functioning autism and Asperger Syndrome in school assessment and intervention.* New York, NY: Guilford Press.

Saunders, D. (2005). *The importance of sensory processing.* Retrieved from http://dsaundersot.webs.com.

Schlosser, R. W., & Blischak, D. M. (2001). Is there a role for speech output in interventions for persons with autism? A review. *Focus on Autism and Other Developmental Disabilities, 16*(3), 170-178.

Schoen, S., Miller, L. J., Brett-Green, B. A. & Nielson, D. M. (2009, November). Physiological and behavioral differences in sensory processing: A comparison of children with autism spectrum disorder and sensory modulation disorder. *Frontiers in Integrative Neuroscience, 3,* 29. Retrieved from http://www.ncbi.nlm.nih.gov/pmc/articles/PMC2776488/

Secor, M. L. (n.d.). *Careers for people with autism.* Retrieved from http://autism.lovetoknow.com/Careers_for_People_with_Autism

Slutsky-Murray, C.M.B., & Paris, B. A. (2005). *Is it sensory or is it behavior?* Austin, TX: Hammill Institute on Disabilities.

Tomchek, S. D., & Dunn, W. (2007). Sensory processing in children with and without autism: A comparative study using the Short Sensory Profile. *The American Journal of Occupational Therapy, 61,* 190-200.

Vann, M. (2007, November 28) Autistic children have more gray matter in brains. *US News and World Report.* Retrieved from www.usnews.com

Vicker, B. (2004). Using a visual support to enhance WH question comprehension. *The Reporter, 9*(3), 9-10.

Wade, V. (2008). *Active intervention: kinesthetic learning style leavens the lump of student achievement of autistic students.* Ann Arbor, MI: ProQuest Information and Learning Company.

Waner, K., Behymer, J., & McCrary, S. (1992, October). Two points of view on elementary school keyboarding. *Business Education Forum,* 27-35.

Watling, R., Deitz, J., & White, O. (2001). Comparison of sensory profile scores of young children with and without spectrum disorder. *American Journal of Occupational Therapy, 55*(4), 416-423.

Weismer, E. S., Lord, C., & Esler, A. (2010). Early language patterns of toddlers on the autism spectrum compared to toddlers with developmental delay. *Journal of Autism and Developmental Disorders, 40*(10), 1259-1273.

William, D., Goldstein, G., & Minshew, N. (2006, August). Neuropsychological functioning in children with autism: Further evidence for disordered complex information-processing. *Child Neuropsychology (Neuropsychology, Development and Cognition: Section C), 12*(4-5), 279-298.

Williams, D. L., & Minshew, N. J. (2010, April 27). How the brain thinks in autism: Implications for language intervention. *The ASHA Leader*.

Winner, M. (2005). *Strategies for organization: Preparing for homework and the real world.* Retrieved from www.socialthinking.com

Winner, M. (2007, July). Teaching organizational skills to individuals with autism. *Autism Digest.* Available from www.socialthinking.com

Suggested Readings

Baranek, G. P. (2006). Sensory experiences questionnaire: discriminating Sensory features in young children with autism developmental delays and typical development. *Journal of Child Psychology and Psychiatry, 47*, 591-601.

Bloom, L. (1988). *Language disorders and language development.* New York, NY: MacMillan.

Brown, N. B. (1998). *The relationship between context and sensory processing patterns in children with autism.* Lawrence: University of Kansas, Occupational Therapy Education.

Buron, K. D., & Wolfberg, P. (2008). *Learners on the autism spectrum.* Shawnee Mission, KS: AAPC Publishing.

Dills, C., & Romisczowski, A. J. (1997). *Instructional development paradigms.* Dubuque, IA: Kendall/Hunt *Publishing* Co.

Koomar, J., & Friedman, B. (1992). *The hidden senses: your balance sense.* Rockville, MD: American Occupational Therapy Association.

Kranowitz, C. (1998). *The out-of-sync child: Recognizing and coping with sensory integration dysfunction.* New York, NY: Skylight Press.

Mackay, G., & Shaw, A. (2010, January). A comparative study of figurative language in children with autistic spectrum disorders. *Autism, 14,* 29-46.

McIntyre, S. (2010). *Handling sensory integration disorder at school: Strategies to ease the stress of sensitive children.* Special Needs Parenting, Suite 101. Retrieved from http://suzanne-mcintyre.suite101.com/handling-sensory-integration-disorder-at-school-a211555

Paris, B. A., & Murray-Slutsky, C. (2005). *Is it sensory or is it behavior?* New York, NY: Psychological Corporation.

Ramachandran, V. S., & Oberman, L. M. (2006, November). Broken mirrors: A theory of autism. *Scientific American,* 63-69.

Whitby Schaffer, P., Travers, J. C., & Harnik, J. (2009). Academic achievement and strategy instruction to support the learning of children with high functioning autism. *Beyond Behavior, 19*(1), 3-9.

Williams, M. S., & Shellenberger, S. (1996). *How does your engine run?: A leader's guide to the alert program for self-regulation.* Albuquerque, NM: Therapy Works, Inc.

Appendices

Appendix A

Overview of Research on the Brain, ASD, and the Writing Process

As mentioned at the beginning of this book, the human brain is a very complicated machine. Recent brain research has shown that there are some significant differences in the way the brain functions in individuals with ASD. These differences often contribute to difficulties in the language, organization, sensory, and motor skills needed for writing. Throughout this manual, based on current research, we have attempted to explain why individuals with ASD struggle with various aspects of writing. Medical research is steadily increasing our knowledge and understanding of the link between brain functioning and the writing process. As new research is completed, we will continue to grow in our understanding of the link between brain functioning and writing. And with that growth in knowledge will come an increased ability to support individuals with ASD in the writing process.

Listed below are a few selected pieces of current medical research that have given insight into why individuals with ASD struggle with writing.

Brain Functioning

Ability to Focus Attention and Solve Problems: Ramifications for Writing
The Howard Florey Institute (Australia's leading brain research center) found that children with ASD have less activation in the deep parts of the brain responsible for executive function (attention, reasoning, and problem solving). "Specifically, we found that activity in the caudate nucleus, a critical part of circuits that link the prefrontal cortex of the brain, is reduced in boys with ASD" (Howard Florey Institute, 2005).

Ability to Imitate Motor Movements: Ramifications for Writing
Manzar Ashtari, a senior neuroscientist at Children's Hospital of Philadelphia, found differences in gray matter in brains of persons with ASD. This difference was especially evident in the mirror neurons of the parietal lobe. These mirror neurons, sometimes called the "monkey see, monkey do" cells, help the brain imitate the motor movements of another person (Vann, 2007).

Difficulty Moving Motor Skills From Being a New Skill (Cortex) to an Automatic Skill (Cerebellum): Ramifications for Writing
Researchers at Johns Hopkins School of Medicine found that the brains of individuals with ASD had significantly fewer neural connections between the cortex (where new skills are processed) and the cerebellum (where automatic and planned motor skills are stored). This would suggest difficulty in moving new motor skills into long-term,

automatic memory (Mostofsky et al., 2009). It is estimated that 80% of children with ASD have difficulty with motor tasks, including writing with pencil or pen. In this study, typical children showed greater brain activity in the cerebellum. The children with ASD displayed more brain activity in the supplementary motor area, which is needed to plan an action such as when one is starting to walk or when attempting to write.

Poor Communication Between Parts of the Brain: Ramifications for Writing
Dr. Martha Herbert (Herbert et al., 2004), an assistant professor of Neurology at Harvard Medical School and a pediatric neurologist at the Massachusetts General Hospital, led a study that indicated ASD brains have more white matter but much less communication between parts of the brain and, therefore, less integration of information (i.e., organization).

Implications of Brain Research for Treatment of ASD: Ramifications for Writing
Williams, Goldstein, and Minshew (2006) reported that highly structured behavioral interventions that focus on one skill at a time may not be effective in developing long-term growth of individuals with ASD. Because their brains do not efficiently communicate newly learned information with other parts of the brain, information that is learned in a highly consistent, structured setting may not transfer to the real world.

Ability of the Brain to Organize and Communicate Information to Other Areas of the Brain During Sentence Comprehension Tasks: Ramifications for Writing
Researchers at Carnegie Mellon Center for Cognitive Brain Imaging and University of Pittsburgh School of Medicine found a significantly lower degree of information integration and synchronization across the large-scale cortical network for language processing in individuals with ASD (Just, Cherkassky, Kellar, & Minshew, 2004).

Ability of the Brain to Efficiently Process and Integrate Sensory Input: Ramifications for Writing
Researchers at the Children's Evaluation and Rehabilitation Center at Albert Einstein College of Medicine of Yeshiva University found that when children were presented with sounds and other sensory stimuli, those with ASD displayed a deficit regarding the speed with which they were able to process and integrate the multisensory input. As a result, they had to use much more effort to process sensory information at a multisensory pace ("Autism research finds ...," 2010).

Impact of Sensory Input on Cognitive and Emotional Processing: Ramifications for Writing
Our cognitive and emotional processing relies upon accurate sensory input. A lot of teamwork has to occur. When we take in information from one of our senses, it is also routinely interpreted by other senses (Greenspan & Wieder, 1998). This can pose problems for individuals with ASD, many of whom have sensory issues.

Development of Gross- and Fine-Motor Skills: Ramifications for Writing

Jasmin and colleagues (2009) found that children with ASD had large delays in gross- and fine-motor skills compared to typical children. Another study assessed motor skills in young children 21-41 months. All of the children in the study with an ASD had delays in gross- or fine-motor skills or both (Provost, Lopez, & Heimerl, 2007).

Ability to Form Letters: Ramifications for Writing

Bastian, Fuentes, and Mostofsky (2010) compared 14 typical children and 14 diagnosed with mild autism. They found that the children with autism had much more difficulty with the quality of forming letters due to poor motor skills. However, they did not show a difference with regard to the size, alignment, and spacing of their letters.

Gender Differences: Ramifications for Writing

Several studies of brain functioning indicate that even though girls and boys with ASD may have similar cognitive abilities, their ability to manipulate language may be significantly impacted by their gender (Burman, 2009; Howell, Davis, & Williams, 2008; Kimura, 2000). For example, girls have greater brain activity in several known language areas:

- Girls had more brain activity in the inferior frontal gyrus on both sides of the brain (an area especially involved in word meanings and other language functions).

- Girls had more brain activity in the superior temporal gyrus on both sides of the brain (an area especially involved in the sounds of words).

- Girls had more brain activity in the fusiform gyrus on the left side of the brain (an area especially involved in the spelling of words and their visual identification).

- The language-related brain activity in girls was on both sides of the brain whereas the activity in boys was only evident on the left side (Burman, 2009).

Sensory Processing

Sensory-related strategies are included throughout this manual to provide the foundation for successful writing to occur. Here is why.

Sensory integration, simply stated, involves the ability to take in, sort out, and process the sensory information we receive from the environment around us in an organized manner. We think of having five senses, but actually we have seven senses: Visual, auditory, olfactory (smell), taste, tactile (touch), proprioception, and vestibular. The last two are our "hidden" senses. Proprioception and vestibular involve our sense of body position and our sense of movement (Miller, 2006).

Sensory Processing/Proprioception: Ramifications for Writing

Our sense of proprioception provides us with information regarding where our body parts are in relation to each other, where we are in space, and where we are in relation to our surrounding environment. In order for us to move, it also relays messages regarding the intensity with which we need to contract our muscles (Miller, 2006). For example, when we are attempting to write, it is our sense of proprioception that supports the ability to functionally sit at a chair and desk, to use just the right amount of pressure when holding a pencil, as well as pressing the pencil to paper to form letters while the nondominant hand stabilizes the paper with just the right amount of pressure.

Our sense of proprioception also has a great impact on calming and internally organizing, including using deep pressure touch or heavy work activity (Murray-Slutsky & Paris, 2005). So if you have had a great massage or participated in some resistive exercise, you benefit from your sense of proprioception.

Sensory Processing/Vestibular: Ramifications for Writing

Our vestibular sense provides us with a sense of movement. The vestibular receptors are located in our inner ear and travel in two directions: up to the cochlea and the visual system and down to our proprioceptive and tactile systems. Our vestibular system provides us with information about balance, movement, and gravity. For example, the vestibular sense tells us if we are moving, which direction we are moving, and how fast. It tells us right side up from upside down. Vestibular input provides information about our head control, eye gaze, muscle tone, posture, and even the coordination of using both sides of the body. The vestibular system is also involved with our sense of balance (Murray-Slutsky & Paris, 2005). Our vestibular sense works to provide a physical reference that can assist with making sense of visual information. When we attempt to write our vestibular system has a huge impact. We need to be able to hold our head and neck up against gravity while writing and write with one hand while stabilizing the paper with the other. Our eyes and hands need to efficiently work together. Even the spacing needed between letters and words, all of this is impacted by the success of our vestibular system.

Our vestibular system also has an impact on our level of arousal (our level of attention and focus), thus influencing our nervous system. The vestibular system directly feeds the reticular activating system, the part of the brain that is responsible for maintaining a level of alertness. The vestibular system works with the proprioceptive and tactile systems, which provide students with an awareness of how their bodies are moving through space and with their coordination (Murray-Slutsky & Paris, 2005). Keep in mind that the vestibular system is activated with movement, so …

- To wake up: Fast movement
- Calming: Slow movement
- Organizing movement: Linear and forward /backward movement (such as jump on a trampoline, use of a glider)
- Rotary movement such as spinning in circles can have an alerting effect but sometimes has a disorganizing effect

Vestibular input can last up to six hours, depending on the intensity, frequency, and duration (Saunders, 2005).

Sensory Processing/Learning: Ramifications for Writing

Research has shown that sensory processing also affects a student's ability to learn (Ayres, 1979; Bennett-Brown, 2008). Approximately 70% of our behavior is based on how we process sensory information. In a study of 200 children with an ASD, 94% displayed unusual sensory processing patterns, including auditory processing, motor planning and sensory modulation disorder (Greenspan & Wieder, 1998). Another study noted that as many as 90% of those with an ASD may experience sensory processing dysfunction (Leekam, Nieto, Libby, Wing, & Gould, 2007; Schoen, Miller, Brett-Green, & Nielson, 2009).

Dr. A. Jean Ayers, PhD, OTR, is the pioneer of sensory integration. Through many factor analytic studies, she identified sensory processing dysfunction in tactile, vestibular, proprioceptive, and visual systems that interfered with language, motor planning, cognition, and emotional well-being (Murray-Slutsky & Paris, 2005). The intent of providing sensory-based strategies (Ayers, 2000) is to assist the child in reaching a calm alert state; this is when we are at our maximum ability to successfully function within our environment. This well-regulated state is referred to as "homeostasis." During homeostasis there is an internal stability, which allows us to respond appropriately to both external and internal stimuli. Our cognitive and emotional processing is reliant upon accurate sensory input. A lot of team work has to occur. When we take in information from one of our senses, it is also routinely interpreted by other senses (Greenspan & Wieder, 1998).

Many students with ASD and sensory challenges seldom reach homeostasis. However, by seeking out the appropriate sensory-based activities, they may be able to increase their comfort level and time engaged in an activity (Murray-Slutsky & Paris, 2005). In particular, the vestibular, proprioceptive, and tactile systems are very powerful, which may help a child to reach a calm alert state.

> Sensory strategies that involve weighted deep pressure input such as the use of a weighted vest, weighted blanket, weighted lap pad, or pressure vest should be evaluated and guided by an occupational therapist trained in sensory processing and, therefore, is not included in this manual.

Sensory Processing/Patterns With ASD: Ramifications for Writing

Tomchek and Dunn (2007) used the Short Sensory Profile to compare the sensory processing patterns of 281 children with ASD to those of age-matched peers who were typically developing. These researchers found that 95% of children with ASD showed some degree of sensory processing difference, with the greatest differences reported in the areas of Underresponsive/Seeks Sensation, Auditory Filtering, and Tactile Sensitivity sections.

Similarly, Watling, Deitz, and White (2001) found that children with ASD differed from their typically developing peers on 8 of 10 subcategories on the *Sensory Profile*, including Sensory Seeking, Emotional Reactive, Low Endurance/Tone, Oral Sensitivity, Inattention/Distractibility, Poor Registration, Fine-Motor/Perceptual, and other categories.

Appendix B

Glossary

Mention of the following terms in the text is marked by an asterisk.

Assistive technology: The Individuals with Disabilities Education Act (IDEA; 2004) describes assistive technology as "any item, piece of equipment, or product system … that is used to increase, maintain or improve functional capabilities of individuals with disabilities." Assistive technology (AT) supports for writing can be as simple as a pencil grip or as high tech as a word prediction software program to support language and spelling.

Bilateral integration: Involves the coordination between the right and the left side of the body. Bilateral integration enables a student to write with one hand while stabilizing the paper with the other.

Brain Gym®: Brain Gym® movements, exercises, or activities refer to the original 26 Brain Gym movements, sometimes abbreviated as "the 26." These activities recall the movements naturally done during the first years of life when learning to coordinate the eyes, ears, hands, and whole body. The 26, along with a program for learning through movement, were developed by educator and reading specialist Paul E. Dennison and his wife and colleague, Gail E. Dennison; www.braingym.org

Bubble wrap: Bubble wrap refers to sheets of bubbled plastic used to protect items during shipping. It may be purchased at office supply stores. Bubble wrap can be placed on a student's chair to sit on. The air movement provided through sitting on the bubble wrap may give the student the movement he is seeking without getting up from his chair. It also may challenge his posture, helping him to attain an improved position for writing.

Chunk information: "Chunking" means to break down information or an assignment into smaller segments so that it is more manageable for a student.

Close-point/far-point copy: A close-point copy is a visual support that is placed on the student's work surface, very near his point of writing. A far-point copy refers to print that is at a distance from the student's desk. A daily agenda written on the chalkboard is an example of a far-point copy, whereas a daily agenda placed on the student's desk, within a few inches of his writing, is an example of a near-point copy.

Desk and chair size: For appropriate seating and posture, the student should be able to rest his feet on the floor. The desk height should be 2 inches above the elbow when the elbow is flexed at 90 degrees. Proper seating can make a positive difference in the quality of a student's writing.

Fidget: A small object that can be held, squeezed, or manipulated by a child to help him remain calm and focus his attention. Fidgets are often used to help individuals with sensory processing difficulties release anxiety and satisfy the need for movement. Frequently used fidgets include things like a koosh ball, a keychain, a stress ball, or a small toy.

First /Then Card: A simple visual cue that visually explains to an individual what he is to do or what will be happening and what will follow. It may be a preferred activity or a reward that follows after the student completes the task.

Example:
First, reading

Then, swinging

This can also be visually shown as (a) what is the task, (b) how much the student has to do, and (c) what he is supposed to do once he is done.
1. Take out paper and pencil
2. Write five sentences about your pet dog
3. When you are finished you may read your favorite book

Functional pencil grasp: For young students, using small crayons and pencils matching the size to their hands may facilitate the formation of a functional tripod grasp (thumb, index finger, and middle finger positioned on the pencil, see illustration).

Golf pencils: These are short, small pencils such as those used for scoring when playing miniature golf.

Graph paper: Paper with small ruled squares that is often used for printing, graphs, diagrams, and math. It comes in various-sized squares. Graph paper can be very helpful for size and placement of letters. The student can also leave a square empty to represent leaving a space between words.

Graphic organizer: A graphic organizer, sometimes called a mind map or concept map, is a visual way of organizing ideas. A graphic organizer for paragraph writing can be a simple web design of a center circle with lines coming out of the circle. With this type of graphic organizer, the student writes (or draws) a keyword in the center circle representing the main idea (or topic sentence) of his paragraph. On each of the lines coming out from the circle, the student writes (or draws) a keyword representing a detail relating to the topic sentence. These cues are then used to organize the sentences of a paragraph. A more sophisticated form of graphic organizer resembles a visual outline or flow chart. In each instance, the purpose of the graphic organizer is to help the student visualize and organize his ideas as he prepares to write.

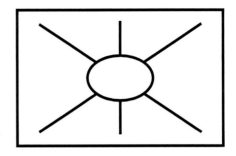

Hand-over-hand support: To offer hand-over-hand support, gently place your hand over the back of the student's hand. Provide gentle support to the student to help him initiate the writing process. Hand-over-hand support may also involve placing your hand over the student's nondominant hand to support stabilizing the paper.

Heavy work activities: An activity that provides push, pull, lift, or carry calms and organizes the student internally, assists with attention and focus, and provides important information to his upper body to assist with the tone, visual motor, and motor planning needed for printing. This can include …
- Taking a crate of books to the school office secretary or media center
- Delivering two plastic jugs of water to the cafeteria
- Doing 20 wall push-ups or seat push-ups
- Following up with slow, deep breathing

Multisensory: A multisensory teaching method helps students exercise several areas of their brain as they learn spelling patterns, including auditory, visual, and motor. When students are asked to incorporate the spelling words into writing tasks, multisensory learning yields greater probability of carry over of correct spelling. Other multisensory strategies include …
- Air drawing, spelling in shaving cream, sand, beans, even salt.
- Forming letters on a vertical dry-erase board while standing and moving
- Clapping, snapping, patting legs as you spell words
- Jumping during spelling
- Singing the spelling words

Peer buddy: A classmate who is paired with a student with a disability as a way to promote social interaction, foster social skill growth, encourage communication, and promote positive behavior modeling. Peer buddies may be same-age students, or they may be older students who function as mentors. Peer buddies may serve primarily as social contacts, or they may be trained to provide academic peer-mediated instruction (see below).

Peer-mediated instruction: An evidence-based practice in which peers are trained to provide tutoring in educational, social, and/or behavioral areas (Chan et al., 2009).

Personalized spiral-bound journal: The idea is to create a writing journal for a left-handed student. The journal is bound on the right-hand side rather than the traditional left side. The traditional left metal spiral binder blocks the left hand, causing discomfort and poor quality of printing.

Many schools have access to a binding machine. It creates the holes in the paper and then feeds the plastic spiral into the paper. If this is not available, merely take 10 sheets of appropriate paper and staple one corner. This will allow the student a better outcome by not being bothered by the metal binder.

Pencil grip: A variety of pencil grips are sold commercially. Typically, the pencil grip fits near the end of the pencil to assist the student with a functional grasp on the pencil for efficient writing. The pencil grip should encourage a tripod grasp, which involves the thumb, index finger, and middle finger positioned on the pencil. For students who use a functional tripod grasp (see Functional Pencil Grasp) on a pencil but hold it too high or too close to the lead of the pencil, try using a small pencil grip that is round and fits over the pencil providing visual and tactile input but does not require the tripod positioning.

Scaffolding: An educational strategy in which the adult provides a framework that allows a student to focus on a specific part of a task. For example, if the student is working on organizing ideas into a paragraph, the teacher might provide transition words such as *first/second/next/then/finally*. As the student becomes more proficient with the targeted skill, the scaffolding is reduced.

Scented pencil: These writing tools provide various scents while writing. For example, a pleasant scent may assist with calming and focus for writing (https://www.smencils.com/original.html).

Story frame: A writing support designed to help the student focus on selected skills in content, structure, or mechanics. The adult provides a framework for the story or paragraph, and the student is asked to fill in the blanks by providing the targeted content, structure, or mechanics.

Storyline: A visual support for creative writing. Much like a timeline, it helps sequence ideas and events into a logical order. It is different from a timeline in that it allows the sequence of ideas to be determined by imagination and plot rather than strictly by time. For example, sequence for a storyline might reflect the thoughts and behaviors of multiple characters rather than a strict adherence to what happened first, second, third, etc. When used with students with ASD, the adult may write keywords (or draw simple pictures) representing the student's ideas on a horizontal line, providing organizational support for the student. The student is then able to write his story, using the storyline as a visual support.

Stretchy exercise band or tubing: The bands are flat sheets of thin elastic rubber, usually six to eight inches wide. Tubing is natural rubber tubing. Both can be used to tie on to two of the legs of a student's desk. The student can receive sensory input with his lower legs and feet with the bouncy resistance of the band for sensory regulation (www.therapband.com).

Systematic phonics: Systematic phonics instruction includes any method that follows a carefully selected sequence of letter-sound relationships that are organized in a logical order.

Talking word processor: Talking word processors are software programs that read the words aloud as a student types. Most talking word processors can be set so that they read one word, one sentence, one paragraph, or one page, depending on the needs of the student.

Text reader/text-to-speech/talking word processor: Text-to-speech software reads computer print aloud. The student can highlight what he has written, and the computer then reads his written work out loud. The student can also highlight, email, and hear it read aloud. Many (but not all) websites can be read by a text-to-speech software. Examples of text-to-speech software include *Read:Outloud*, *Write:Outloud*, and *Word Q*. These and other commercial products are described in Appendix H. **Note.** Text readers/text-to-speech software/talking word processors are different from voice recognition software (see below).

Visual timer: A visual timer helps the student to understand the concept of "how much longer." It teaches the student how much time has passed. The student can "see" the time without truly being able to tell time. Visual timers help with setting time limits, assist with tolerating transitions, and facilitate being present in working within a time frame. The entire class may benefit from the use of a visual timer. A free visual timer may be downloaded from www.online-stopwatch.com or www.online clocktimer.com. Commercial visual timers are available from www.timetimer.com or www.therapyshoppe.com.

Voice output device: Also known as speech-generating devices (SGD) or voice output communication aides (VOCA), these devices are most often used by individuals with limited speech abilities. The device is programmed with sounds, words, or phrases to help the individual communicate his thoughts and needs. *Go Talk* (gotalk.com) or *Talk Pad* (www.rehabengineer.com) are examples of voice output devices. Other options are listed in Appendix H.

Voice recognition software (also known as speech recognition software): With voice recognition software, an individual speaks into a microphone, the software converts his voice into text, and the text appears on the computer monitor. The student can then highlight the text and hear it read aloud. This type of software can be especially helpful for students whose verbal abilities are much higher than their writing abilities. *Dragon Naturally Speaking* is one example of voice recognition software. Several other commercial products are available (see Appendix H).

Word prediction: Word prediction software anticipates the correct word after an individual types two or three letters. A list of possible choices appears on the monitor. With each letter the individual adds, the list becomes more specific. Many word prediction programs have a text-to-speech function whereby the computer speaks the word aloud. A frequency function is also included, with frequently used target words appearing after only one or two keystrokes (see Appendix H).

Word wall: Word walls are literacy tools used mostly in elementary school classrooms. As part of a reading instruction program, teachers designate one wall (or part of a wall) in the classroom for displaying commonly used vocabulary and/or sight words in large print so that all students can read the words from their desks. The students can then refer to the wall during literacy exercises. The large visual nature of word walls helps students to naturally gain familiarity with these high frequency words, as well as to gain reinforcement of vocabulary.

Appendix C

Tips for the Left-Handed Writer

Left-handed writers frequently cover the letters and words they have just created as their left hand moves across the paper. This makes it difficult to see how much space to leave between words. Try the following to help remedy such situations:

- Keep a spacing tool (see Appendix F) close by to monitor the spacing between words.

- Provide a three-ring, three-inch binder turned in a horizontal position. This will provide an elevated slanted writing support. This position will raise the paper for improved viewing and positioning of the left hand.

- Provide the letters or words that you are expecting students to copy from the paper on the right side of the paper. Students writing with their left hand spend a lot of time lifting their hand to see any text their hand covered that they should be attending to.

- Flip a spiral notebook over and have the left-handed student start from the back page for journal writing. The typical metal of the spiral on the left side of the paper can be annoying. When the notebook is flipped over, the metal spiral is now on the right-hand side.

- Teach students to position the paper to the left of the midline of their bodies. Tilt the paper with the top right corner of the paper positioned closer to the student than the top left corner. Many students develop strong habits early on. Encourage the child to remember to keep his arm perpendicular to the bottom of the paper. Ideally, the student's wrist should not be flexed.

The wrist should be straight (not bent), and the writing hand should be *below* the writing line.

Appendix D

Letter Formation Strategies

Use a variety of materials to help students learn to form letters correctly. Build a strong motor memory of the letters **before** paper and pencil writing.

The following are all hands-on strategies; no paper or pencil is involved.

Wikki Stiks (Amazon.com:wiki sticks): Create letter shapes using different colors of Wikki Stiks. (They resemble long pieces of candlewick in various colors. They stick on mirrors and most surfaces.) The student can help create and also feel the finished letter.

Play dough: Roll out letter shapes with fingers; pinch, pull, and squeeze.

Salt: Place a layer of salt in a pie pan or small tray. Model for the student the correct letter formation in the salt. The student follows by forming letters correctly in the layer of salt.

Sand: Place sand in a shallow tray with sides. Model correct formation of shapes and letters and have the student practice.

Shaving cream: Have the student help squirt out shaving cream on a hard surface, spread it out, and then use finger to create shapes and letters.

Wood puzzle pieces: Create letters from part to whole with wood shapes or hard styrofoam pieces. Straight and curved pieces of wood or styrofoam are useable. Model for student practicing capital letter formation. The program *Handwriting Without Tears* sells wooden pieces for letter formation (www.hwtears.com).

Air writing: Create letter shapes with finger drawing in the air. The teacher models, tracing with finger in the air, on the floor, or a tabletop.

Letter shapes: Form letter shapes and glue them onto paper out of any of the following:
    Small cereal pieces
    Yarn
    Small shells
    Buttons
    Macaroni shells

Chalk: Create letter shapes with chalk on a vertical chalkboard or sidewalk.

Hair gel in a plastic zip lock baggie: Trace letters with finger on the outside of the bag of gel.

Magnetic letters: Use on a cookie tray or pie plate to practice forming words.

Rubber stamps of letters with inkpad: Create letters using letter stamps. This is a great way to practice letters and words and also good for strengthening the skill side of the hand needed for good writing.

Hand/Finger Strengthening Activities

Legos, Tinker Toys, and Bristle Blocks: Push together and pull apart to build fine-motor strength and coordination.

Putty: Squeeze, mash, pull, and pinch to build fine-motor strength and coordination.

Scissors: Scissor cutting activities strengthen the skill side of the hand.

Paper tearing: Tearing paper into small pieces and making a collage by gluing torn pieces to a picture can be a fun activity that encourages many fine-motor skills.

Tongs or tweezers: Picking up cotton balls and dropping them in a bucket can be a fun way to build hand coordination.

Tennis ball with a slit cut for a "mouth": The student can squeeze the "mouth" open with one hand as he "feeds" coins into the slit with his other hand. This is an excellent activity for building two-hand coordination.

Appendix E

Letter Writing Tips

- Provide opportunities for prewriting activities in order to build skills. Remember that a child's ability to trace over a shape, color within the boundary, copy a "I - O / +, triangle," and draw a simple picture forms the building blocks for prewriting skills for writing letters and words. Provide opportunities for a multisensory approach to letter formation. This involves visual, auditory, kinesthetic (movement), and tactile experiences.

- Overemphasize to the student to start letters at the top.

- Practice letter formation at a vertical dry-erase board or chalkboard.

- Try air drawing with fingers in the air to form letters providing kinesthetic (multi-sensory) feedback. Start with large shoulder movement with letter formation by air drawing and forming letters on the dry-erase board.

- Set up sensory motor stations for teaching letter formation (see Appendix D). This may include the use of small metal pie pans with sand, a station with shaving cream, a station with play dough, or a station using hair gel in plastic sealed baggies. Combine the auditory component with the tactile sensation and movement of the finger as the student forms the letter. The student may then feel the line as he moves his finger through shaving cream provided on a tray. He may hear and say an easy chant such as "start at the top, big line down." The student sees the line in the shaving cream. He may even smell the light fragrance of the shaving cream creating a calming feeling while working on printing skills.

- Consider the use of a research-based handwriting program such as *Handwriting Without Tears* (www.hwtears.com).

- Whenever possible, use the child's preferred activities when learning to form letters. For example, if the student enjoys trains, when teaching the letter "b" say, "The **train** starts at the top of the track, goes down, back up, and around the track." Or for letter "r" for a student who is interested in sharks, "The **shark** dives down into the water, swims back up to the top, and then swims across."

- If possible, move from manuscript to cursive writing the last semester of second grade or as the student is moving towards third grade, dependent on the student's personal profile. Manuscript letters traditionally are made from the top to the bottom. Cursive letters traditionally are made from the bottom to the top. This bottom-to-top movement is easier for some students. Additionally, cursive writing eliminates the start/stop movement of creating separate letters, thus eliminating some of the spacing challenges. There is also natural spacing between words when using cursive. Each student is unique. Remember to consider all of your student's strengths and challenges, including developmental level, when deciding to continue to work on printing or when it is appropriate to introduce another strategy.

Appendix F

Spacing Between Words

The following is a list of various types of "spacing tools."

- Use a wooden clothespin. Ask the children to draw eyes, nose, and mouth on it. For fun, they can call their character "space boy" or "space girl." When students use their tools consistently, it doesn't take long for appropriate spacing to become a habit.

- Let the children glue a "google" eye on to the clothespin. Tell the students this will help them to keep an "eye" on their spacing as they place the spacing tool between their words.

- Create a visual. "Leave a spaghetti-thin space between letters in a word." "Leave a meatball-size space between words in a sentence." Or use another visualization that has meaning to him.

- Leave a finger space between words. This is perhaps the simplest strategy. The student places his index finger after each word, starting the next word after the finger. In the beginning, repeating the phrase "new word" is helpful when encouraging the student to leave a space.

- Modeling spacing between words for the student is very helpful. Over-space to emphasize the space between words. Try letting the student draw a line between the words that you have modeled for him.

- There are commercially available products that support spacing between words, but using an eraser, tongue depressor, or paper clip as a visual to space between words can work just as well.

Appendix G

Keyboarding

The power of technology is embedded in many of the strategies presented here. As with any instructional tool or strategy, it should be carefully looked at per individual student, grade level, and abilities. Keyboarding skills are an important component for all students in the 21st century. In addition to increasing the ease of writing, researchers (e.g., Hoot, 1986) have found that elementary students who learn to type achieve greater gains in reading comprehension, vocabulary, word study, and spelling skills. Students in first grade who had participated in a reading/typing program scored significantly higher than the control group on understanding paragraph meaning, word study skills, and spelling skills on the *Stanford Achievement Test*. Students were also found to have improved independent reading, listening, and organizational skills. In addition, their attention span improved.

When keyboarding, a student does not have to worry about making a letter correctly. Students who experience eye-hand coordination problems often become frustrated when their writing is disorganized, poorly spaced, and poorly formed. When the finished product is legible, clear, and readable, a student's confidence and self-esteem benefit. When confidence increases, a student's interest in writing may also increase. Finally, keyboarding skills may help with organization and improve eye-hand coordination and the ability to self-correct work.

For first or second graders, to "hunt and peck" at a computer keyboard is appropriate, as they are becoming familiar with a new tool. Typing skills may not be functional for many as they are unfamiliar with a keyboard. Initially, the keyboard may be used to practice spelling words or short assignments to gain familiarity. Students soon make the connection of the ease with which they can create a letter, erase through a simple key stroke, and clearly read what they have produced.

It is recommended that a keyboarding tutorial program be introduced in third grade. Studies have found (e.g., Fleming, 2002) that eight years old is a good age to start, because by then students have generally developed the coordination and manual dexterity required to keyboard efficiently. It is also an age when writing demands increase considerably in school. Keep in mind that for some students with ASD, the fine-motor skills may be delayed and keyboarding skills, therefore, may need more time to develop.

Directed practice several times per week will increase keyboarding proficiency and support writing skills. Students tend to follow the keyboarding tutorial more accurately when adult supervision is present and encouraging to the student. Discourage hunt and peck by fourth/fifth grade. Bad habits may begin to form, making learning appropriate keyboarding skills more challenging.

"Automaticity" means to be able to do something without conscious attention. According to Bloom (1986), over time, people develop skills that turn into an automatic process. Walking, jumping, skipping, swimming, ironing, stirring a mixture, drawing, dancing, driving, and running are examples of skills that often become an automatic process. Keyboarding can also become an automatic process. Waner, Behymer, and McCrary (1992) agreed with Bloom, pointing out that in order for keyboarding to be beneficial to the student, automaticity is required. To develop good touch-typing skills, students need to learn at an early age. A minimum of 10-15 minutes three times a week is recommended for a keyboarding tutorial. Four to five times a week is even better.

Types of Keyboards

Various keyboards are commercially available, such as a standard keyboard, portable word processor, or even an adaptive keyboard for individuals with special needs.

The standard keyboard layout used with computers and laptops is called the QWERTY layout. However, there are a number of keyboards on the market to support special needs. Keyboards are available with large keys, high-contrast color keys, special layouts, and with a trackball, these can all help increase computer accessibility (www.especial-needs.com/computer-aides-keyboards).

Free Online Keyboarding Tutorials

Here are some websites with free keyboarding tutorials. Practice 3-5 times per week for 10-15 minutes.

http://www.sense-lang.org/typing/
http://www.powertyping.com/
http://www.nimblefingers.com/
http://www.typingsoft.com/all_typing_tutors.htm
http://www.typingweb.com/
http://www.goodtyping.com/
www.kidsdomain.com/brain/computer/type.htl
www.http:/files.uberdownloads.com/apps/tuxttyping/index.php
www.typingweb.com
www.bbc.co.uk/schools/typing/ http://www.abcya.com/keyboard.htm
http://www.keybr.com/
http://www.jonmiles.co.uk/fingerjig.php
http://webinstituteforteachers.org/~gammakeys/Lesson/Lesson1.htm
http://www.usspeller.com/keytutor.html http://www.powertyping.com/rain.shtml http://
www.powertyping.com/baracuda/baracuda.htm
http://www.typingmaster.com/individuals/bubbles.asp
http://www.bbc.co.uk/schools/typing/
http://www.goodtyping.com/
http://funschool.kaboose.com/fun-blaster/games/game_type_me.html
http://www.senselang.com/ http://www.typeonline.co.uk/lesson1.html
http://www.typing-lessons.org/
http://www.learn2type.com/
http://gwydir.demon.co.uk/jo/typing/index.htm

Appendix H

Assistive Technology Writing Support

Software

Many of the software programs listed below provide multiple features. For further information, refer to the individual websites.

Type of Software	WEBSITE	DESCRIPTION
Graphic Organizers		
Draft:Builder	http://www.donjohnston.com	(Mac/Windows) Guides students through three steps in creating writing drafts: organizing ideas, taking notes, and writing the draft.
Inspiration	http://www.inspiration.com	(Mac/Windows 98-7) Assists students with visual mapping and provides outlining tools to assist in creating mental models. A free trial may be downloaded from http://www.inspiration.com/Freetrial
Kidspiration	http://www.inspiration.com	(Mac/Windows 98-7) Provides a semantic mapping tool for K-3. (We have used it with older students with developmental delays.) It features text-to-speech feedback and a visual library to support visual learners to organize their writing.
Authoring Tool Software		
Buildability	http://www.donjohnston.com	(Mac/Windows) Provides students with a multimedia authoring program for creating single-switch early literacy activities for books and presentations; features text-to-speech feedback and easy animation.

Type of Software	WEBSITE	DESCRIPTION
Clicker 4	http://www.cricksoft.com	(Mac/Windows) Provides word grids to assist students in creating full sentences with picture graphics, words, and phrases to support writing for beginning writers.
Intellipic Studio	http://www.intellitools.com	(Mac/Windows) Multimedia authoring program tool and easy animation. It provides a variety of activities for all grade levels and content. Curriculum activities, paint and drawing tools, video, sound, and image importing, and animation tools.

Word Prediction Software

Co:Writer	www.donjohnston.com	(Mac and Windows) May be purchased separately or as part of *Solo* (see below). This word prediction program allows the student to type two or three letters and then choose his word from a pop-up list. Operates on a frequency system, with frequently used words appearing after only one or two keystrokes; has the ability to speak each word aloud. Struggling spellers can greatly benefit from this software.
Solo	www.donjohnston.com	(Windows and Mac) Software suite that includes four programs, a text reader, and a great researching tool (*Read:Outloud*), graphic organizer (*DraftBuilder*), talking word processor (*Write:Outloud*), and word prediction (*Co:Writer*), which can function together or separately.

Type of Software	WEBSITE	DESCRIPTION
SoothSayer	http://newsite.ahf-net.com/soothsayer/	(Windows XP or higher. Not available for Mac) Word prediction software; also offers a complete set of speech tools to read text.
Text Help Read & Write Gold	http://www.spectronicsinoz.com/product/texthelp-read-write-10-gold	(Windows and Mac) Provides a full toolbar, including powerful word prediction. This program also assists the struggling speller and picks up spelling errors.
Word Q	www.goqsoftware.com	(Windows and Mac) Reads aloud any text that can be highlighted. Includes a word prediction program. Is often paired with *Speak Q*, voice recognition software, to allow an individual to switch back and forth between typing and speaking his text.

Speech-to-Text Software

Type of Software	WEBSITE	DESCRIPTION
Dragon Naturally Speaking	www.donjohnston.com	(Windows and Mac) A speech recognition system that, as the student speaks, converts speech into typed text. It increases the writing productivity for the student who struggles with paper-and-pencil writing. It currently provides 99% accuracy. It has a new quick voice formatting, which makes it easier to format, delete, and cue words or passages with only the use of a single command.
SpeakQ	http://www.goqsoftware.com/product-details/speakq/	A voice recognition software that plugs into *WordQ*. Requires *WordQ*.
Free Online Speech Recognition	avedelete.com/7-best-free-speech-recognition-software.html#.UFo0Uq7YH-Q	This website provides a description of speech recognition programs that may be downloaded for free.

Text-to-Speech

Type of Software	WEBSITE	DESCRIPTION
Intellitalk 3 – Part of Classroom Suite	http://www.intellitools.com	(Windows and Mac) Full talking word processor and word prediction program with speech options for letter, word, sentence, and paragraph feedback. Formatted to work with Intellikeys and single switches. (Intellikeys is an alternative keyboard designed to support special needs.)
Kurzweil 3000 Version 13	www.kurzweiledu.com	(Windows and Mac) Text-to-speech software. It supports writing, reading and test taking and study skill tools.
Pix Writer	www.pixwriter.com	(Windows and Mac) Supports beginning, challenged, and writers with special needs. Just type in words, and *Pix Writer* automatically creates word bank buttons. Then students can simply click buttons to write; gives immediate speech feedback. PreK-5.
Read: Outloud	www.donjohnston.com	(Windows and Mac) May be purchased separately or as part of *Solo* (see below). The student is able to highlight and move text for future organization into a report or essay.
Tool Factory Word Processor	http://www.toolfactory.com	(Mac/Windows Vista, XP) Talking word processor; allows dragging and dropping pictures, videos, and audio. Hundreds of pictures are available; word bank easily accessible at all times.
Write:Outloud	http://www.donjohnston.com	(Windows and Mac) Complete talking word processor. It will speak by letter, word, sentence, or paragraph. Provides spell check and talking dictionary and bibliographer.

Type of Software	WEBSITE	DESCRIPTION
WYNN	www.enablemart.com/Catalog/Writing	Open a file, and *WYNN* reads aloud or allows the user to scan hard copy documents and have them read out loud.
Writing With Symbols	www.writingwithsymbols.com	(Windows. For Mac a virtual PC program needs to be installed) http://www.microsoft.com/mac/products/) This is a word processing program that can display symbols or other graphics (or text)for each word that is typed. Also reads back to the student. Great for student writing and creating social stories.
Text-to-Speech Free Downloads	http://www.ilovefreesoftware.com/26/articles/10-best-free-text-to-speech-software.html	This website provides information on text-to-speech free downloads.

Communication Devices

Go Talk	www.gotalk.com	Though this is a speech-generating device, it can also be used to record step-by-step directions for a student to listen to and follow for a writing task.
Talk Pad	www.specialed.us/autism/assist/asst14.htm	Though this is a speech-generating device, it can also be used to record step-by-step directions for a student to listen to and follow for a writing task.
Portable Word Processors	www.greatschools.org/special-education/assistive technology	Portable keyboard, lightweight device that functions as an alternative to a laptop for writing. This website describes several portable word processors and their functions.

Appendix I

Sensory Supports for Positioning and Regulation

- **Soft cushion:** A soft cushion may be supportive to a student who has difficulty sitting on the hard surface of a desk chair. Even a rolled jacket placed vertically on a chair can provide tactile input to support sitting. Sitting on some small-bubbled bubble wrap is another option to give the student a wake up (when a bubble pops) while sitting.

- **Move 'n' Sit Air Cushions (http://www.backinaction.co.uk/move-n-sit):** Air cushions provide postural support as well as either wake-up and calming input for students who appear tired and lethargic or students who are having difficulty sitting still.

- **Beanbag chairs:** When the student is sitting in the beanbag, it should be snuggled around him to provide calming deep pressure touch. As his nervous system is calmed and organized, his attention to the writing task may increase. Stabilize the beanbag chair against a solid support or wall.

Appendix J

Treats Are More Than Rewards

Here are some suggestions for choosing a snack during a writing period (or any time) to assist with attention. We frequently offer a food treat as a reinforcer or reward for good work, but a snack may also support the student in achieving his goal. Did you know that our mouths have more tactile nerve endings per square inch than we have anywhere else on our bodies?

Our tactile system has a direct impact on our level of alertness. What we chew, taste, suck, and swallow can have an effect on calming and alerting us. Many students with an ASD are under- or over-responsive to various foods. Though one student may not like the flavor of a tart lemon candy, another student may love it.

Note. *As always, please remember to take individual student needs, in terms of health, safety, and preferences, into consideration when selecting from the following. When in doubt, consult an occupational therapist.*

Chewing provides resistance/organization	
Gum	Granola bar
String cheese	Fruit rollup
Gummi candies	
Crunchy snacks may help with waking up and increase attentiveness	
Crackers	Raw vegetables
Pretzels	Popcorn
Nuts	Apples, raisins
Bread stick	Crushed ice
Sour treats are alerting and organizing	
Lemon candy	Sour ball
Lemonade	
Spicy treats are also alerting	
Atomic Fireball candies	Cinnamon candy
Peppermint candy (can also be calming)	"Hot" crunchy snack
Spicy tortilla chips	
Sucking is internally organizing/calming	
Piece of gum	Lollipop
Cup of ice chips	Water through a straw

What Others Are Saying ...

"This book is a gold mine for anyone working with students with ASD who are struggling writers. The authors address specific writing concerns in an easy-to-understand fashion and offer strategies in the form of templates, graphic organizers, and other structures. As educational consultants, we love the short explanation that accompanies each strategy of why a given concern typically emerges. We cannot wait to put *I Hate to Write* into the hands of teachers as well as occupational therapists and speech-language pathologists. In a user-friendly way, this resource provides the structure that both teachers and students can use every day. The glossary and appendices are an added bonus, with a wealth of information on assistive technology, relevant websites, handwriting tips, and other valuable topics. Fantastic!"
  – Elisa Gagnon, ASD consultant, Blue Valley Schools, Overland Park, KS; and
    Linda Hickey, educational consultant, Blue Valley Schools, Overland Park, KS

"*I Hate to Write* is a must-have resource for supporting any individual who is struggling with the task of writing. There is no other book on the market of this kind! Cheryl Boucher and Kathy Oehler have seamlessly combined their respective disciplines to offer effective and practical strategies that will teach standards-based writing skills, thus increasing student achievement. Easy to use, the book is loaded with solutions and activities for virtually any writing challenge. This is an invaluable resource for teachers, therapists, and parents alike."
  – Megan Ahlers, director of Exceptional Learners, MSD Pike Township,
    Indianapolis, IN; and Colleen Zillich, autism consultant, Southside Special
    Services of Marion County, Indianapolis, IN; co-authors of *The Classroom
    and Communication Skills Program: Practical Strategies for Educating Young
    Children With Autism Spectrum and Other Developmental Disabilities in the
    Public School Setting*

"As an educational consultant working with school districts, it is great to have a resource for learning to write aligned with the National Common Core State Standards and evidence-based practices. This book does an excellent job of describing the 'why' of the multiple facets involved in the skill of writing. The authors give hundreds of strategies to help teach writing to students who hate to write in the area of motor, language, sensory, organization, and technology. Teachers everywhere will like the ready-made activities and worksheets. I recommend that all teachers have this remarkable resource for their classrooms."
  – Melissa Dubie, educational consultant, Indiana Resource Center for Autism; co-author of *Intimate Relationships and Sexual Health: A Curriculum for Teaching Adolescents/Adults With High-Functioning Autism Spectrum Disorders and Other Social Challenges*

"Have a reluctant writer in your classroom? If so, you need this resource-rich book from two educators who clearly know what it takes to support students on the spectrum. Their 'take it and use it' activity pages will be helpful not only for students with autism labels but for any learner in your classroom, including your strongest and most enthusiastic writers. This is a collection of tools for K-12 classrooms that no writing teacher will want to be without."
— Paula Kluth, PhD, author of *"A Land We Can Share": Teaching Literacy to Students with Autism*

"*I Hate to Write* has an easy-to-read layout that speaks to the concerns of teachers and therapists equally. It addresses teacher concerns related to National Common Core State Standards. From a therapeutic standpoint, it provides research in an accessible format to explain the whys of the concerns while offering a large variety of strategies to address the language, organization, sensory, and motor aspects of each concern. The information regarding program software and websites for handwriting interventions is comprehensive, well organized, and pertinent to each concern. The visual support outlines and recommendations are top-notch and teacher/therapist-ready-to-use. This is a wonderful resource for better understanding the ASD brain, particularly as it relates to writing challenges. It offers rich information to better our skills to support students with autism to reach and demonstrate their full potential in the academic setting."
— Rita Magdowski, OTR/L, Livonia Public Schools

"Cheryl Boucher and Kathy Oehler tackled a HUGE issue for students with autism spectrum disorders and WON! This no-nonsense reference addresses common teacher concerns with insight and creativity so that learners are engaged and successful. From letter formation to the use of technology and reinforcements that increase learning, there is something for everyone in *I Hate to Write*! No more tears and meltdowns over writing assignments—I can't wait to share this with all of our families."
— Sherry A. Moyer, MSW, LSW, executive and research director, The University of Toledo Center for Excellence in Autism

PUBLISHING

P.O. Box 23173
Shawnee Mission, Kansas 66283-0173
www.aapcpublishing.net

CPSIA information can be obtained at www.ICGtesting.com
Printed in the USA
LVOW050330020413

327119LV00001B/1/P